Who Knew?

Michael Ray

Daisy Lane Publishing/Daisy Lane Inspirational

Copyright © 2021 by **Michael Ray**

First published in Australia in 2021
By Daisy Lane Publishing/Daisy Lane Inspirational

All rights reserved. No part of this publication may be reproduced, distributed, or transmitted in any form or by any means. This includes any means graphic, electronic, or mechanical, including photocopying, recording, taping or by any information retrieval storage system without prior written permission of the copyright owner except in the case of brief quotations embodied in critical articles and reviews.

Although the author and publisher have made every effort to ensure the information in this book was correct at press time, the author and publisher do not assume and hereby disclaim any liability to any party for any loss, damage, or disruption caused by errors or omissions, whether such errors or omissions result from negligence, accident, or any other cause.

Cover Design © 2021 Carolyn De Ridder

Who Knew?/ Michael Ray. -- 1st ed.

ISBN: (sc) 9780648771876
ISBN: (e) 9780648819332

Dedication

Se non fosse per la mia famiglia sarei niente
The luckiest bloke in the world to be born into this family.
And to my incredible daughter, Charlie, you inspire me
to be better every day.

"Sometimes it's the princess who kills the dragon
and saves the prince" ~ Samuel Lowe

And finally, to my incredible partner Robin who is my superior in
every way, and without who this book wouldn't exist.
You make our lives better in every way.

Acknowledgements

If you have picked this book up in the belief it was some sort of parenting advice manual, here's some of the most valuable parenting advice a mug like me can give you. Put it down immediately. Back up to the bookstore assistant and ask for anything by Maggie Dent, the 'Queen of common sense.' This amazing person and the work she does managed to resonate, guide, and even calm this nervous, first-time, know nothing dad in a way that actually made me believe I could do this parenting gig, and not give myself some sort of stroke from stressing about it.

While I am happily dispensing proper, useful wisdom, others - not mine, do yourself a favour and seek out Craig Harper's, 'The You Project' podcast. I can see people, even Craig, quizzically looking at me and wondering what has Craig's field of expertise in self-management got to do with being a parent? One of the many realisations, or 'Who Knew?' moments, was the realisation that I shouldn't judge my parenting on my daughter's behaviour. After all, I was lucky enough to have the easiest kid in the world. I needed to judge my parenting on my own behaviour and as such I needed to be better because it's no longer just about me. As parents and as humans, we need to develop and grow just as our children do, and parenting has been the greatest self-development catalyst I could have ever envisaged. *Who Knew?*

In the journey through life, and if you are lucky – which we have established I am – you get to meet some truly exceptional individuals that fight the good fight, that are champions of causes and slayers of dragons, and without the support and reporting of these exceptional individuals. Dr. Susie O'Brien, Herald Sun journalist, social commentator, and author of the fantastic, 'The Secret of Half-Arsed Parenting' (available through Murdoch Books) my story really would never have been told.

Standing on the precipice of my new career, I was once again lucky to meet someone that was willing, and dare I say eager to give me that very needed push in the right direction. Rachel from Kiddipedia gave me the first opportunity to publish some of my writing. She has been a staunch supporter and cheerleader every step of the way.

While I'm thanking people and there are so many that have been integral to easing my insecurities around not being emotionally equipped to raise this kid on my own from the amazing mum tribe who've always had my back to Charlie's Kindy teacher Kay who always made sure there was left over Father's Day presents for Charlie to buy at the Mother's Day stall. These seemingly little things, made a huge impact on Charlie and I. My personal training clients that have known me well before Charlie even arrived, in fact, the same motley crew who have seen me weekly for twenty-three years, definitely need a mention. Without each and every one of you, I would not be able to give Charlie the life and experiences that we are fortunate to be able to afford. Each one of you have contributed to who I am today.

My final thanks go to my family. My Mum and Dad didn't prepare me to be single handedly responsible for raising a little girl of my own, not directly with any real intent or process that is. What my parents did do though, was provide me with a fantastic example of what parents do.

As children we are always watching, and it was through this observation that the foundation for my values were laid; a sort of Jedi mind control teaching the way of parenting. To my sister Leanne, for the unwavering support, family BBQ's and swimming, sleep-overs and fabulous coffee's when we visit. And to my brother, lost too soon, every silly, wild and crazy thing that Charlie and I do together reminds me of our childhood together; it reminds me that although someone may not be here in body, they will always be here in spirit. The memories that I am creating with Charlie will hopefully mirror the memories that I have of Tony and me.

My OTHER final thanks – this will be the last – is to all of those that have somehow found interest in what I have to say. TV appearances, radio interviews, podcasts and seminars from around the world – especially my UK tribe. The absolute best thing about the space I am in is hearing the stories about the amazing relationships and memories created by so many fantastic fathers. In my eyes, this is the only legacy that matters.

My dead set, LAST and final thanks is to The George's at The Informer TV, Australian TV legend, George Donikian and George Hazim, both all-round top blokes, for affording me the opportunity to be a regular social commentator on their show.

Disclaimer

This book is a compilation of stories, media releases and podcasts penned by myself about my journey into parenthood. These pages are personal opinions and interpretations and memories, and as we know opinion, interpretations and memories all have their own stories to tell.

Everything I've written is true but may not be completely factual. I've added my elucidation on events that may differ from other recollections, but I've always loved a good story. I may have changed a few names and character traits to protect some people.

I've quoted some studies in which you will find reference to at the end of this book. I have also quoted a few brilliant individuals and some parenting legends, however, this does not make me a parenting guru – these pages are just my musings, my thoughts and my reflections.

I hope you enjoy them.

Foreword

By Maggie Dent

Over the last few years, I have read many of Michael Ray's articles nodding in agreement and I found his light hearted style of writing easy to read while being deceptively full of insight and wisdom. His ability to capture real moments from family life were raw and honest and often his perception through the eyes of a loving dad, helped me appreciate how it is to be a dad.

Until Charlie was born, I had no idea that a love so intense could ever exist, an all-consuming overwhelming mix of fear of the unknown, a sense of such intense pride that it sometimes makes my heart feel like it's going to explode.

One of the most fabulous cultural changes happening in our world is around fathering. Finally, fathers are being embraced as capable, caring parents who can 'mother' children. Everywhere from playgrounds, to schools, to community events and online we are witnessing dads stepping forward with tender hearts and genuine love. There are wonderful podcasts helping dads decode being hands on parents with tips on choosing baby carriers, how to store breast milk effectively in the freezer and how to get babies and toddlers to sleep.

The award-winning cartoon Bluey has been a wonderful fun resource that for once shows a dad who is present, committed and loving instead of an incompetent buffoon. This is long overdue.

Michael Ray was your atypical Aussie bloke – a former bouncer and body builder and yes, his muscles are big and real. He came from a long line of dads – and unexpectedly had a life-threatening wake-up call that brought him to realise that he needed to change and step up and be the best dad he could be for his precious daughter. His stories will have you cringing at times, others crying, and there will be laughing and many moments of asking why? Michael embraces imperfect good enough parenting and shares some of his less than perfect fathering moments to show how these moments can become valuable teachable moments for everyone!

Michael Ray is a voice that needs to be heard. In his writings he explores the areas that challenge modern dads with common sense, humour, and concern. From his story about being banned from helping Charlie backstage at the dance concert – until he challenged the rules, to having no change tables in men's toilets and being excluded from parent rooms! Then there is the Maternal Child Health Centres and why maybe they need to become Parental Child Health Centres as up to 1 in 7 dads are found to struggle with postnatal depression.

There are so many truisms that Michael shares that we can all embrace as parents and one of my favourites is 'the quality of your attention is love.' When do you offer your child your total presence? I especially love Michael and Charlie's focus on Sundays as being their day of connection. He also explores the notion of micro-connections as well as macro-connections and some of them are when doing family chores like cooking, making school lunch and the bedtime chat before sleep. The love notes in Charlie's lunch box story has the most magical heart warming response from Charlie over time. I shed some good tears with that one.

As this cultural change continues its way through the Western world, we need to review societal norms that are often expressed without thought. Michael mentions ones like 'a girl needs a mother', 'a maternal instinct' or 'mother knows best.' As the numbers of solo dads increase we need to be mindful because a paternal instinct can be a positive thing too. Dads with partners can also struggle with these messages. Healthy attachment is what babies, toddlers and children need and the gender of the caregiver does not have to be an issue. Michael is raising his daughter to know she is loved without conditions and to make sure she knows her own worth and value. Every parent wants this surely?

Gradual systemic and structural changes are needed to allow dads to become a valued part of positive contemporary parenting. When outdated gender expectations keep both men and women from embracing parenting, everyone suffers, especially children.

Who Knew? will give everyone food for thought and it will lift your spirit and leave you full of hope that we are all in this together – raising all our precious children in our communities surrounded by caring parents and caregivers both men and women.

Thank you Michael for sharing your story, your thoughts and your truth.

Maggie Dent

Parenting author and educator and host of ABC Podcast Parental as Anything.

www.maggiedent.com

Contents

Introduction 1

Who Knew? The Beginning 11

Chapter 1 23

Chapter 2 35

Chapter 3 51

Chapter 4 69

Chapter 5 81

Chapter 6 97

Chapter 7 111

Chapter 8 125

Chapter 9 135

Chapter 10 149

Chapter 11 155

Chapter 12 169

Phat Fatherhood Facts 181

Charlies Chapter 189

References 193

About the Author 197

Introduction

"Who knew that the *gift* of clarity would hit me square between the eyes, bestowed upon me through a crisis that would see me re-emerging as a better human, not disconnected from my pre-crisis self, more as though I had been shattered into a thousand pieces and suddenly, completely, and permanently reassembled into a sentient and grateful dad."

Michael Ray

Random quote, I know. So, let me expand. It had it's beginning in an accidental crisis, one that I'm forever grateful for. Even if in my juvenile male manner of dealing with crisis, I reverted to gung-ho humour and smart-arse retorts to deal with the news.

It all culminated and came crashing down one night. My personal life was in shambles. My health was suffering physically and mentally, and my energy levels were at an all-time low. It was completely understandable though, right?

I had been working like a mad man to provide for my new family and wanting to be the best, most hands-on dad EVER. I wanted to be involved in all the minutia of raising my daughter. I absolutely loved everything about it — the night feeds, the nappy changes, bath time and bedtime, because that's what a good dad does, right? A real man, a real dad, puts his family first and any thought of seeing one of those doctor thingy's would just have to wait. (insert alpha male chest pounding and grunting here!)

My relatively short, although important, relationship with my six-month-old daughter's mother had ended a couple of weeks earlier and in that time, I hadn't seen my daughter who I'd waited my entire forty-nine years to be blessed with. Strange, isn't it? Forty-nine years without this kid and suddenly a day apart from her was almost unbearable.

I decided that I needed a night out; a distraction to drag me out of the dark recesses of my mind. Adding some alcohol seemed like the perfect route to the resolution of my physical and mental malaise, right? (insert more chest pounding and grunting here)

And what a good night it turned out to be. In fact, it was that good it didn't end for a couple of nights as was the fashionable trend of my excessive youth. But like all good things, they must end. I found myself waking up in a haze at a stranger's house and after a full day and into the evening of awkward, trivial conversation, biding my time to ensure I was sober enough to flee. I got into my car and started my trip home.

As I listened to the great tunes, slowly the temporary distance I had put between myself and my thoughts dissipated. I let reality pour over me with my attention suddenly snapped back to the present and the dog in my path. The 'don't swerve' advice that is recommended was forgotten. As a lover of animals, there was no way I was going to add to my brilliant list of failures by killing a helpless animal. I hit the brakes. The dog froze in the headlights, like a deer. There was no stopping now and there was only one option that didn't involve a dead or damaged dog. I swerved. BANG! I hit a tree.

I swear the dog was laughing at me, and life, once again, was giving me the middle finger, or vice versa, maybe even both. The dog hastily departed the scene without the slightest pretense of going for help, as was the legend of the much-revered Lassie.

The tree was conveniently located directly across from a convenience store and not so conveniently lodged firmly in the front of my car. The dear souls on duty witnessed the whole accident and called for an ambulance. After much arm waiving, bad jokes, and reassurances that I was fine, I relented and decided to get a free ride to the hospital. After all, my car was not going anywhere, and I had lost any hope the dog was returning to promise me that his first-born son would be named in my honour for saving his ungrateful life.

After being quizzed, prodded, poked and breathalysed, I arrived at the hospital and was wheeled off to wait for the inevitable cursory examination. With my obvious extensive medical knowledge, gathered from years of near miss hospital visits and selected TV medical shows, led me to conclude with relative certainty, that the examination was indeed unnecessary and I would soon be released, with me carrying a sense of guilt for wasting everyone's time to add to my list of growing achievements.

While lying, waiting, my mind had decided now was the perfect time to compile a chronological highlight reel of every failure, stupid decision and self-inflicted near-death experience I had made throughout my colourful and eventful life, complete with narration by someone who sounded incredibly like Morgan Freeman — alas, it was not he.

The initial vigour and flurry had died down and I'd been downgraded from emergency to a simple procedural check-up after 'concerns' were quelled by the attending physician. I was lying in the hospital room, surrounded by the silence of an early morning hospital, waiting for the CAT scan. In the silence, one tends to get lost in the valleys of the mind, you wonder around and look behind rocks and trees that you'd forgotten, or rather, had chosen to forget. I was still trying to come to terms with the separation of my marriage and not having seen my six-month-old daughter for what seemed like an eternity but in reality, was only a few weeks.

I will admit, on the surface, my best efforts at portraying that I was in good spirits was a façade that was hardly manageable even though I had been taught my entire life, 'Never let your opponent know you're hurt', and despite having spent a lifetime practicing and developing my male bravado I was suddenly feeling weak, even a little vulnerable. I felt a tiredness that ran so deep it was hard to breath and it made my heart beat with a deafening rhythm that was reminiscent of a boxing match's final round. I was completely gassed, unable to even hold my hands up to protect myself from my opponent's punches. Blow after blow landed as I stood in front of him like a punching bag with eyes. I took great comfort, even pride in the fact I wouldn't buckle or show any weakness to him or the crowd of spectators, yet here I lay in the quiet of the hospital scared, filled with a sense that life hadn't quite managed to knock me out, but had managed to punch me into submission. I wanted to quit. I felt that I was buckled and my ego, my pride, my bravado had thrown in the towel and deserted me.

It was an uncomfortable and confronting feeling. A lifetime of squashing everything down into that pit had suddenly exploded from the depths like an inflating raft, except this felt like it was going to drown me, rather than save me.

Looking back at this time, especially with the benefit of hindsight and my gift of clarity that this unfolding crisis had endowed me with, I lay there thinking about my daughter. To this day, thinking about Charlie makes me well up with emotion. Charlie, who was named after my dad, really was perfect to me, yet, somehow in the instant she came into this world, I knew intrinsically, and without doubt, I had to be better than the carefree Peter Pan that I had been until now. I'd had a colourful life — a life that makes my Mum blush and shake her head in disbelief. From being a burly bouncer and doorman by night, providing security for almost every local and international rock star that travelled to Australia; a bodybuilder and personal trainer by day, living it up in Melbourne's 80's and 90's. Being from this clique one realises that this lifestyle is one of fanciful excess granting complete disregard for the future. You think you're invincible, unstoppable, bulletproof.

I was brought back to the future by a nurse who wheeled me in to have my CAT scan, a precaution I was told just to make sure that my neck was okay. There was no internal damage. As I waited for the doctor I began to think about how this was another lucky escape like the other near misses I'd had.

The scan was simple and painless, but I'd had enough. I really just wanted to crawl into my own bed and get a good sleep before my day needed to start again.

I walked out and caught a cab home.

I was in a deep sleep, enveloped by my warm blanket, when I became aware of a tiny but frantic voice calling my name accompanied by a tapping. The tapping got louder as did the voice, now bellowing my name. I woke up with a start, sitting bolt upright in my bed. Mum was standing in my doorway, pale and panicked.

"Michael," she scolded, "I've just got off the phone with the hospital. What is going on? They said you walked out. You need to go back. They're sending an ambulance!"

I woke fully at the word ambulance. I told mum to get my sister so she could run me to the hospital to see what all the ho-ha was about. Bless my sister's soul, she's a good egg and did her sisterly duty of driving me and stopping for coffee and breakfast first.

After the flurry of paperwork and evil sideward glances from the nursing staff, I was shepherded in to see the doctor. He looked grave and serious, so serious in fact that my sister was asked to leave the room.

Once alone the doctor informed me that I was going to be admitted and required to stay for a week after telling me how lucky I was. Obviously, I had no clue what he was talking about. In my style, I mentioned something about this not being Club Med and that the coffee was sub-par.

He raised his eyebrow and proceeded to tell me that the Bilateral Pulmonary Embolism was his major concern and nearly the end of me. That it would have been me cashing in my ticket. So, if that was the major concern, what on earth were the minor concerns? I didn't have to wait long for a response.

They still had to assess to see if it was a surgical procedure or simply treatment that I required. The fact that the embolisms – yes, I did say embolisms – plural, were well formed and residing happily in my lungs, was the reason they wanted to keep an eye on me. Touch and go according to the professionals.

Apparently, the good news was that when these were addressed and treated, they would then proceed further to investigate the masses found in my brain, nodules in my lungs and the lymph node abnormalities. Besides that, I was in great health.

My sister eventually came back into the room after the doctor left to find me in a complete daze. There was sudden clarity. I had been feeling short-of-breath and generally under the weather, but I would never have guessed that this would be the issue. I honestly thought that I was just getting old and my carefree and happy life until now was taking its toll. It felt like the soundtrack to my life was beginning to end. For all my jokes and quips, I was scared; really scared.

After all, becoming a father so late in life was in itself a shock and until Charlie was born, I had no idea that a love so intense could ever exist – an all-consuming, overwhelming mix of fear of the unknown, and a sense of such intense pride that it sometimes makes my heart feel like it's going to explode. It's almost as though my life before was of no real consequence or significance, just all-in preparation.

With Charlie's mum and I ending our relationship coupled with the days that I'd not seen Charlie, the uncertainty of how this split would affect this newfound purpose and now the given diagnosis, it was safe to say that I was in crisis. My focus was drawn acutely onto what really matters versus the stories I'd been telling myself for years about what I thought mattered, was the *gift*.

My world had, in a split second, become my house that I'd built, furnished and filled with a lifetime of effort, and in an instant there's flames leaping through the roof and I had to consider what, if anything, was I prepared to rush in to try and save. What was replaceable, expendable or of no consequence? How much of my life, my energy and focus had been used up in acquiring these things?

Most people, when I ask this question, reply with photos, keepsakes, basically memories of a life connected to others and experiences.

And therein is the *gift of clarity* that sadly, many times only comes from crisis. Life is so much easier for me with a strong, clear, and authentic set of values to give me a governing motivation and perspective for life.

At forty-nine and becoming a dad, my male bravado disappeared in a flurry of nappies, bows, and pretty dresses. I've never felt so vulnerable and unsure, more scared about the measles, scuffed knees and snot noses with the possibility of not being able to protect against broken bones and hearts!

WHO KNEW?

Who Knew?

The Beginning

"I look at the way my daughter looks at me.
I see how she is always watching for how I respond to life
and its challenges. I see how she laughs at my lame dad
jokes. I see how she loves me unconditionally and how,
frighteningly, she wants to be exactly like me.
In short I am HER hero."

Michael Ray

I'm often asked how I became an advocate for equality and change, and my standard answer is, 'quite by chance.' There was certainly no conscious decision that set me off on this path. I would never have professed, predicted, or even dreamed that I would somehow be considered a 'woke' new age bloke. In fact, if anything, I would have more likely been described as a dinosaur. Coming from a place of scarcity and still slightly in disbelief that I had become a father, my main concern was to maximise my time and have as much fun with Charlie as possible before she went off to school. I had the best little adventure buddy a Dad could ask for.

One of the fun activities we enrolled in was ballet. As with all little ballerinas, the hours of jetés, pliés and other fancy French ballet words for jumping about with your mates, culminated in the end of year concert which was of particular excitement for me. If you had told this big, tough, ex-bouncer that one day he would be backstage at his three-year-old daughter's ballet concert, struggling to contain his nerves and completely failing to hold back his tears of pride, I would have laughed at you. (possibly thrown you out of the pub!) But there I was, with one job as a priority and that was to support my daughter – my sudden case of emotional incontinence would have to wait. Apart from Charlie's birth, this was the most emotionally charged event I had ever been a part of and I had once won a wheelbarrow of chocolate in grade two!

In the lead-up there was the usual doubts, nerves, tears and there may even have been a tantrum or two, and that was from me. Thankfully, with Charlie's support, encouragement, and example, I was able to make it through the concert with only minor weeping and major whistling, whooping and cheering. At this stage Charlie still thought I was cool and smiled and gave me the thumbs up.

So, when the next year's concert rolled around, Charlie filled with enthusiasm and me armed with a pocket full of tissues to cry into, continued our foray into the magical (tear stained for dad) world of performing arts excellence that is 4-year-old ballet classes and somehow, I finally felt like I was just one of the parents until …

> **THEATRE REHEARSAL**   Friday November 18
> - Please supply correct undergarments, footwear, tights and hair accessories
> - It is recommended that mothers wait throughout this rehearsal.
> - Upon arrival - enter via the front door/ foyer
> - Normal dance class uniform to be worn
> - Mothers will be able to watch portions of this rehearsal (upon invitation)

We excitedly received all the information regarding the end of year concert. The information was full of 'mothers' this and 'mothers' that – no biggy I thought – a simple oversight; even a standard letter that hadn't been checked perhaps? After all, I'm used to changing mother to father after reading to Charlie every night at bedtime.

Studies show that fathers continue to be portrayed as less involved and more invisible than mothers in the world of their children. Books, magazines, and morning television shows are filled with information about and for mothers and mothering.

With information pack in hand and ready to laugh at my misconstrued interpretation of the information, I headed off to the ballet school to attend the pre-concert information session, excited to clear up any issues and to purchase the 'Mummy and Me' ticket.

> ***SPECIAL OFFER FOR OUR TINY DANCERS!!*** Tickets $40.
> We have a special *Mummy and Me* ticket discount to encourage our Tiny Dancers to watch and enjoy our show with an adult (for either show in which they are not performing).

With a flurry of activity and excitement all of us 'Mums' gathered in the hall for the pre-concert briefing which was a read through of the supplied information pack and to dispel any pre-concert jitters.

I sat quietly in the hope that it would come to someone else's attention that there was an actual father within their midst and that they would point out the oversight contained and reviewed in the information pack and of course amend 'mothers' to 'parents' — after all we were knee deep in our rainbow socks in the marriage equality debate in Australia and the awareness and acceptance that families and love come in all different shapes and sizes and had never been higher in my life-time.

The devastation when I was told that it was certainly no printing error, no oversight, and was, in fact, the standard practice that was in place, and it served the school well up to this point and they could see no need to change it just for me. I pointed out that these stipulations were not mentioned at the previous year's concert.

> **DRESSING ROOMS**
> - Dressing rooms will be divided and clearly marked with individual class names.
> - No males are permitted into the dressing room at any time.

The ballet school asked me some of the very same questions employers had over the years.

Can her Mum do it? Does Charlie have an Auntie or a Nanna to do it? Could you arrange for someone Charlie knows to look after her? I had one answer to all of their questions —

"I'm a single parent, Charlie's only available parent and I am 100% responsible for her needs."

I left the meeting in disbelief and with Charlie's little hand curled in mine we walked to the car. I will never forget the look on her face and her asking if I was not allowed to be at the concert. I tried to put her at ease by explaining that it was only that I wouldn't be able to help her get ready in the backstage area.

As I was strapping her into her car seat, several of the Mums came out to let me know that I should fight it and that they thought it was ridiculous as the previous three-year-old ballet concert did not have this embargo placed on it and it was a raging success that was enjoyed by all – and besides, I WAS one of the girls, and they had my back.

I pondered this situation all the way home while listening to the excited chatter from the back seat about makeup and outfits. I kept the internal dialogue going throughout the afternoon. *Was I overreacting? Was I being unrealistic? Was I being selfish?*

It was never about me not being allowed backstage that was the catalyst that necessitated me taking a stand. It was about Charlie being made to feel different from the other children because of our family situation. The thought of Charlie not having my support as her parent to share the excitement and her pride, broke my heart.

It was time to pen the email, the email that would lay out our case and to ask for reconsideration. With a push of a button, I sent it through to the school.

From: **Michael Ray**
Date: Fri, 14 Oct 2016, 5:15 pm
Subject: Charlie Ray and the end of year concert
To:

Dear Miss Jess

I'm writing in the hope that between us we can come up with a mutually acceptable solution to the problem of myself not being allowed as a "male" backstage at the end of year concert.

I'm not sure if you're aware of our situation but it's just Charlie and I in our wonderful little family with Charlie having had no contact with her mother for over two years.

While Charlie has constant hurdles and reminders of the fact that our family situation is different from that of her peers, I try my hardest to minimise the potential harm it may do to her emotional wellbeing and self-esteem.

So hopefully you can appreciate my concern that the potential of the blanket ban on father's being allowed backstage may have on Charlie feeling somewhat different as she would be the only child without the opportunity to share their excitement and nervousness with a parent.

Surely the use of some sort of modesty screens being available or even the other parents being made aware beforehand that because of the wonderful diversity of modern families that it's not fair or possible to impose an unfair and arbitrary ban on families that don't fit the stereotypical definition of a family?

I look forward to working with you to come up with a plan to make this another amazing opportunity for Charlie and the other students to shine.

Please feel free to contact me   or by return email or at class on Thursday morning.

Regards
Michael Ray

Shortly after, I received a polite email offering a private meeting to discuss the matter. The more I thought about it the more determined I became as I could not comprehend any reason for this ban that couldn't be addressed. Tempered by the fear that my persuasive skills may fail and leave Charlie as the only child backstage without a parent by her side to help calm her nerves and share her excitement, I thought it best to not leave the outcome to my somewhat limited negotiation skills. On the suggestion from a couple of the other Mums, I decided to contact the Victorian Equal Opportunity and Human Rights Commission to enquire if this was in fact gender discrimination. They informed me that based on the information supplied that this was most definitely discrimination. They wished me luck and suggested that I keep them in the loop as they may be able to assist me further if required.

One of the mums suggested that I also contact the wonderful Susie O'Brien from the Herald Sun newspaper. Susie made contact with me shortly after I left a message for her. She asked if I would mind if she tried to make contact with the school for comment – which she duly did. I found it a welcome reassurance that I was not being driven purely by my emotions and the fear of failing Charlie.

I spent the better part of the week leading up to the private meeting discussing the issue with a number of people. I really needed to ensure that I was not being emotional or just being the protective parent.

The response was overwhelmingly in support of my position. There were, however, a few that told me that, *'this is just the way it is'* or *'they could understand the school's stance on the issue.'*

Much to my delight, all my fellow 'Dance Mums' voiced their support for Charlie and I to be treated just as any of the other kids and their parents and threatened a boycott if they didn't revise this discriminatory rule.

Thankfully, the school had a change of heart and to this day I am unsure if it was my beautifully penned email, Susie's interest in the situation or the realisation as the bastion of the contemporary arts that they could participate in the unstoppable march towards marriage equality that our country was on and, hopefully, see these outdated gender expectations thrown in the rubbish bin of history.

How can the gender of a parent be an issue as we were about to finally have marriage equality in this country?

Susie O'Brien's full-page story came out in the Herald Sun newspaper and I'm constantly amazed at how far-reaching this story has resonated and echoed with other's experiences. It was covered by all the major networks, talk radio, and even saw us have the opportunity to be featured on a Disney™ website.

The messages of support and encouragement, the letters to the editor and the call-ins to the radio and TV stations was both humbling and unexpected and made me realise that this is obviously not an isolated or unique position I find myself in.

While situation and circumstance has resulted in me having the opportunity and awareness to advocate for others this was only ever about my daughter having the same opportunity as any other child to have their parent present and involved in all aspects in her life.

Happily, at the concert, Charlie excelled in her performance and except for a massive case of nerves (mine), which ended in uncontrollable sobbing backstage (also me), I eventually managed to control myself thanks to the hugs I was getting from complete strangers and my Mum Posse, it was another great night – even if Charlie teased me about the tears - again!

WHO KNEW?

Chapter One

Long Line of Dads

"Rather than fatherhood being limiting as it may appear from the outside, I've found fatherhood has given me the freedom to cast off the ego, façade, and pretense and actually discover who I am as a person and as a man."

Michael Ray

I come from a long line of dads. My dad was a dad, his dad's dad was a dad and his dad's dad's dad was also a dad. See how it goes? However, at forty-nine, I had long ago accepted it wasn't even certain the opportunity to be a dad would eventuate and to be honest, with my looks, awkward personality, and complete lack of any understanding of women, I had to accept it was probably for the best. In fact, if you did a quick survey among the people who knew me, I'm fairly sure I would place behind a cheese sandwich, an odd sock, and a pot plant as a possible last-minute babysitting candidate.

I don't think any of the dad's in this long and unbroken family lineage of dads actually went about any formal preparation, study, apprenticeship or, thankfully, read a book such as this, written by a late starter who somehow stumbled into the role of dad, such as myself. After all, parenting, or at least what I and many others with outdated gender expectations considered the important aspects of parenting, like keeping the kid alive and nurturing them to a level that wouldn't see them one day on the news for torturing small animals, was more the responsibility of Mums.

Dads were seen, at best, as a bumbling, (almost) reliable assistant, possibly the second adult in the room. The idea in the 1960's when I was born, was that a dad could possess a 'parenting instinct' and not just be a provider or a disciplinarian who was often used to invoke children's compliance with the phrase, "Wait till your father gets home," a common refrain for my generation, just wasn't something that was even considered.

In one of the earlier scientific studies dating back to the 1980's on children's early development looking exclusively at mothers, with over

2,000 surveyed into different parenting styles and outcomes, there was not one solitary father in the cohort. However, science is making up for lost time with papers and studies being published almost daily into the unique and important benefits dads provide their kids.

I don't think any of the dads in my long line of dads consciously thought that they were preparing themselves or any of their offspring to become a dad. It seems that we just collected our dad skills (or lack off) through observation. Dad jokes – pull my finger, shoulder rides, all sorts of gravity and death-defying throwing of our kids worthy of a seasoned circus act just magically appeared. Thankfully, these seemingly innocuous interactions between dads and their kids actually have profound effects according to the slew of academic papers arriving almost daily. Children with involved, present dads have better outcomes in behavioural, psychological, educational results and are even less likely to end up in jail. In fact, all of this contemporary research shows that fathers are important for a child's development. *Who knew?*

Parenting tasks such as learning to swim and more importantly how to do an impressive cannonball entry into the pool, learning to ride a bike, climb a tree, kick a footy, hell, even how to stand up to the local bully seemed to be handed down from father to child in our family. Studies have shown encouraging children to take risks, engage in rough and tumble play can help prevent childhood anxiety disorders. Who knew that by encouraging kids in a reasonable way to push their limits that dads could be helping to reduce their child's risk of developing an anxiety disorder?

Despite this lack of training, my dad was my hero when I was a kid. More important, his values and actions are my example as an adult. He was everything I wanted to be; strong enough to open whatever jar mum passed to him; smart enough to always be able to tell when I wasn't quite telling the exact truth of what happened to the last biscuit. His mind reading ability was worthy of a magician.

He possessed super powers rivalled by any comic book hero simply by raising one eyebrow and saying, "really?" was a truth serum more potent than anything James Bond had ever dreamed of. His X-ray vision was uncanny in its ability to not only see into the any room in the house, but to combine it with his usual cry of, "I know EXACTLY what you're doing in there!" could stop my best wrestling leap from the tallest available piece of furniture onto my siblings. He did have one temporary lapse in his superpowers though that allowed my sister to sport what was probably the first ever punk rock hairstyle, years ahead of its time courtesy of myself with my older brother, Tony, assisting.

But did any of this prepare me for the situation I was now in – the sole parent to a completely reliant and vulnerable little girl? After all, my mother ran the household and therefore did the majority of the kid stuff while dad worked his arse off to ensure we as a family had everything we needed and the division of responsibilities worked beautifully for them. It was a fantastic marriage.

However, this completely typical upbringing left me firmly ensconced in the 'Maternal Instinct,' 'Mother Knows Best,' 'Only a Mother's Love' and all of the other fetishized depictions of motherhood school of thought. Hardly helpful and slightly more daunting than the already challenging task of solo parenting already appeared. In fact, these obsessive and outdated depictions of motherhood led me to defer, or at least seek guidance or reassurance on most parenting duties to Charlie's mother when we were still together. Hardly co-equal parenting, more like an assistant which only adds more unfair and unhelpful pressure onto mums who may be struggling with the normal challenges of parenting a new-born, breastfeeding, colic, post-natal depression, sleep deprivation, routine disruptions and all of the other frustrations of the daily tasks of raising an infant.

These frustrations aren't a lack of some mythical 'Maternal Instinct' or 'a flaw in womanhood'; its parenting, yet dads escape the pressure and the curse of expectations. Despite my best intentions to ensure mum had all of the assistance she required while my daughter received the secret sauce standard of care that only mothers possessed as a result of their gender and biology. *Win-Win*? Hardly. In fact, the opposite. Mum carried extra burden. Charlie missed out the unique benefits of a hands-on dad, and most importantly, she was missing out on having an example of the sort of partner she should have as an adult that would enable her to follow her own path authentically without some outdated gender expectation limiting her choices.

As I grew older my relationship with my dad changed. Somehow my dad knew I was ready for this change in the dynamic of our relationship. I still remember at sixteen-years-old, my dad sneaking me into the pub to watch a Muhammed Ali fight under the strict instructions of, "don't tell your mother." My dad, in the blink of an eye, had become my peer and along with that came the realisation and appreciation that my dad was an actual person, somehow less super and more human. He was an embodiment of respect and affection to me and the example of a devoted and committed family man. It was as though I had arrived at the 'Emerald City' and the big green curtain had been pulled back to reveal the 'Wizard of Oz' and his mystical machinations of the 'Yellow Brick Road' that I was setting out on known as life, were exposed. The examples of my father and the environment he curated of our family life suddenly crystalised into lessons and a set of core values that has led me to understand myself and focus on the things that are authentically important to me and ignore the rest.

When I was a child, and even more so now, I thought my dad was brilliant. He could do anything with ease. My dad never made it to high school, yet, he built our house, he built successful businesses, he could fix or build anything with his hands.

Now that I'm a dad, I understand while he could do anything, he took the time to teach me how to do it for myself. While he didn't make it past grade six, he encouraged me and insisted I persevere at school. My dad didn't just build a house; he built a home for his family. He didn't just build successful businesses; he provided for his family and it wasn't my father's hands that did this it was his heart and soul – his purpose.

As a child, I thought my dad was stronger than I could ever be. He could start the mower with one rip of his muscular arm, carry any amount of shopping for mum and hit my fastest cricket bowling over the fence for a six, and out with ease.

Now that I'm a dad, I understand my dad's physical strength was nothing. It was useless and inconsequential compared to the strength he needed to shepherd and support his family through the loss of my older brother Tony after a car accident. I look back at how he managed;

at how he made sure everyone else was coping as best we could. Now that I'm a father, I realise it was his example, his values and commitment to family that gave me the strength, resilience and determination to not give a rats-arse (one of my dad's often used sayings) about stereotypes or stigmas that has enabled me to easily cast off the expectations of others.

Now that I'm a dad, my dad is even more of a hero; his stature in my eyes, in my heart, has grown exponentially. He became my hero without meaning to; he became my hero without realising it; he became my hero because I watched everything he did. He set such a heroic example. That's how it is for us dads. We carry such an important mantle as the influence and example for our kids, we're larger than life, our jokes are funny as all and our cargo-short wearing fashion sense is as universal as it's acclaimed.

Now that I'm a dad, I realise my example is everything!

Dad taught me his staunch discipline. He taught me that failure is not the end of life; rather than denying the validity of my embarrassment or disappointment he taught me it was a natural consequence. He shared the lessons he learnt from failure so that I hopefully would avoid making the same mistakes.

He taught me that feelings are called feelings because you feel them — fairly obvious concept, right? He taught me that feelings sometimes make sense and sometimes they happen for no discernible reason, out of the blue, sometimes in response to a disappointment or violation of my expectations. However, regardless of their origin, internal or external, logical or illogical, every one of my emotions was completely acceptable, but not every one of my behaviours that flowed from them would be, regardless.

Dad always made time for us. He was reliable and always had our trust. My dad was the best cheerleader for us. Sometimes it felt like he was tough on us but he had our best interest at heart. He always cheered us on and encouraged us to be the best we could. He never tried to manipulate or coerce our behaviour. He inspired us with his examples and actions. My dad's examples and actions were grounded in values that last and are universal regardless of circumstance, gender or situation. Values like honesty, responsibility, empathy, respect for others; examples that are timeless and universal that I still use as the guard rails of my life. I make sure Charlie knows we won't always get it right and that we all make mistakes, however, she needs to listen to the truth that's inside herself, that's authentic to her, even when it's difficult or inconvenient, and yes, even when she disagrees with me. If I'm to maintain Charlie's trust my values and beliefs must always be on display through the consistency and clarity of my actions. This is something that I fiercely follow with Charlie. If I say that I will do something or go somewhere there is no way that I do not honour my word because as my Dad taught me, I want Charlie to know that of all the people that are in her life, I will always, and I mean ALWAYS be here for her and will always keep my word.

After all, that is all I really have to give to Charlie and if I fail, trust starts to break down. I want to know that Charlie will expect and demand this from herself and will hopefully pass this on to her children one day if she decides to have a family. Charlie trusts me and follows me not because she must, but because she wants to. Trust is maintained when values and beliefs are actively managed. Connection and respect are everything for us.

My dad never got to meet Charlie, she is named in his honour and there isn't a day that goes by that I don't wish Charlie had memories of her granddad to carry with her through life. Charlie loves to hear stories of my childhood, or the 'olden days' as she calls them. Growing up in the country and recounting my adventures with my dad – catching snakes, riding horses, billy-cart races and the usual mishaps, broken bones and a pet menagerie that Steve Irwin and Moses combined would struggle to wrangle.

More nights than not, at Charlie's insistence, these stories are the last thing she hears after our reading of some Dr. Seuss book on repeat for the twenty-seventh time, so in a way she does know him and I know how much mischief they would get up to together, were he still here. I still smile remembering my dad chasing us and our cousins around with his false teeth in his hand trying to bite us as we all screamed with a combination of terror and delight. The pranks and slapstick humour that elicits the squeals of joy from children and that intoxicating cackle of laughter from babies is the tequila of preference for this old man now.

Now that I am a Dad, I look into my daughter's eyes and I see my dad. I see the total of his life experiences and how they shaped him, because he shaped me. I see all the work he did. I see all the sacrifices he made for his family. I see the examples he set and the values he displayed reflected back at me through a set of sparkling blue eyes that convince me of the existence of pure love, of limitless joy, convince me of the vital importance of time and not wasting it on the negative.

Now that I am a dad, I realise that rather than fatherhood being limiting as it may appear from the outside, or as I thought when I was a child looking at my dad, I've found fatherhood has given me the freedom to cast off the ego, façade and pretense and actually discover who I am as a person, and as a man it's given me a clarity, a sense of purpose and fulfillment. I've come to believe that parenting doesn't change you – it simply reveals who you really are as a person and for every guy wondering if they have what it takes to be a father and for every father wondering if they're doing a good enough job. It's simple. Decide how you want your children to remember you. What stories do you want them to tell about you? *Be that father.*

I look at the way my daughter looks at me. I see how she's always watching for how I respond to life and its challenges; I see how she laughs at my lame dad jokes; I see how she loves me unconditionally and how, frighteningly, she wants to be exactly like me. That's just how it is in the world of dads. We are larger-than-life, we're heroic in nature and funny as all. In short, I'm HER hero, as my dad was mine. I'm HER example. I'm HER example for right and wrong, for strength and compassion, for safety and affection, just as my dad was, and still is, to me.

When society changes the perspective that fathers provide and mothers nurture a paradigm will shift. When fatherhood is spoken about in the same glowing terms as motherhood, the inertia of outdated gender expectations set in a bygone time that has been slowing our march towards contemporary parenting will be broken. When fathers are respected and recognised for the wonderful, unique benefits we bring to our children – the change, the revolution we need, will begin in the home and workplaces and governments will follow to accommodate the workforce. For too long the tail has been wagging the dog! Even the misguided and divisive practice of classifying parents as primary and secondary, or somehow separating 'breadwinning' from 'caregiving', rather than a being a vital part of it.

Have you seen the outcomes for the 20% of children living in poverty? It is culturally harmful and counterproductive, it demeans, disenfranchises, and potentially damages the relationship, not only between fathers and children, but also between mothers and employers. It has also allowed workplaces to be willfully blind, not only to our parental responsibilities, but also to the overriding reason our careers matter.

WHO KNEW?

Thanks dad!

Chapter Two

Daddy's Girl

"If becoming a father doesn't fill you with uncertainty, not only about the basics of keeping your kid safe, nurtured and provided for, but also that deep unsettling worry that you're not a good enough role model for children to emulate or to seek in a partner – because they will, then you must know something I don't."

Michael Ray

With Dad on my mind, I'm reminded that men for too long have been required or mandated to be the cape wearing, problem solving, dragon slayers. However, we are as fathers the example for our children and to portray the false narrative of invulnerability, which we can do without realising, is to set them up for self-doubt and anxiety.

Before we approach any type of action or make any decision, our authentic inner self, our values, must align with our outer life and goals.

How can this happen if we deny the influence of the inevitable doubt, trepidation and social judgement we all experience?

If we never stepped out of our comfort zone we would never find any real growth or change, and at its basic level isn't that what life is about? Isn't that what we aspire for our children?

My dad was brave in my eyes but not the quintessential definition of brave though. The type of bravery I mean is being able to live mentally within the discomfort of uncertainty; continuing to grapple with questions before jumping to answers, and continuing to seek truth beyond social acceptance and the comfort of conformity or outdated gender expectations.

If becoming a father doesn't fill you with uncertainty, not only about the basics of keeping your kid safe, nurtured and provided for, but also that deep unsettling worry that you're not a good enough role model for children to emulate or to seek in a partner – because they will, then you must know something I don't.

As fathers we must step into this doubt whether we think we are capable or not. Bravery is not a quality we are, or are not, born with. It is one that can be cultivated and honed and rather than deny our fears we must welcome them as an opportunity for growth.

> **John Wayne said:**
>
> "Courage is being scared to death – and saddling up anyway." Ten simple words that summarise fatherhood, by a cowboy, so you know they are applicable dads!

Without doubt, the 'bravest' thing I've done as a dad, as a person, is to realise and accept my vulnerability, my fallibility and flaws, and, in fact, the very things that make me uniquely me.

I remember when I was younger, watching my dad. I was thinking fatherhood looked limiting or stifling, however, I've found it liberating and the catalyst for discovering who I am based on my values that I want for my daughter's example. Was I an athlete? A trainer? An entrepreneur? A writer?

All of those labels have an extrinsic set of characteristics attached to them. Now I'm a dad none of those labels take priority. I'm a parent. Not a father. Not a mother. *A parent.*

People become too conscious of what other people think about them and they try to conform to societal norms. These include how certain genders should act. Even the bravest of us experience fear and trepidation.

I always ask, *How can we move beyond the fear that destroys connectedness?*

Bravery is a product of the heart.

To be sure, we must learn to be comfortable with honest vulnerability that people or society might be judging us, and you may question, — *Maybe I'm not as I'm 'supposed' to be?*

This is an immediate impression. It's not fully rational yet. You need to stop yourself from just agreeing to these impressions, so that you can figure out if they are right.

The crucial part is to discern whether the evaluative portion of that feeling makes sense. Yes, they are looking at me. But that's not a big deal. Also, yes. I'm not conforming to social norms — I'm not as I'm 'supposed' to be. *Why does that matter? Why is that bad?*

> "Human's respect those who seek the truth far more than those who claim to have found it."
> Voltaire

I have never understood the rationale that dictates the most masculine, manly, virile thing you can do which is to sire children, yet, you want nothing more than to stay home, nurture and raise those children. Somehow, this is perceived as a feminine trait. I have had both men and women judge me for not being typically masculine – but then what is typically masculine? —*Barbells and Biceps?*

To understand how much that is worth, consider it this way: Can you put a price tag on living your own life? Do you want this for your children's life? If I offered you a certain amount of money to live a certain way for the next five years, how much would you ask for? What if it was for ten years? How much would you ask for then?

Why are you giving your life away for free? Why are you right now doing what 'they' say without charging anything at all?

Bravery doesn't necessarily entail doing something dramatic or astoundingly heroic. On a day-to-day basis many ordinary people summon uncommon courage to overcome both physical and psychological barriers in order to achieve a variety of necessities and goals.

We first need to muster up the willingness to do so. Before we can acquire any habit, or character trait, we must have a strong desire or willingness to do so. Contemplating the alternative, which would be to live in fear or a position of great vulnerability, should provide ample motivation.

When we work to develop bravery, we both empower ourselves with the ability to confront problems head on, as well as acquire the skills required to deal with life's inevitable challenges and by showing our children our true selves rather than some all-knowing super heroic depiction of masculinity. We set the example.

Men have been endowed with the gift of speech even though we don't use it nearly as much as we should. We must use this 'gift' wisely. And when our hearts and minds authentically combine around an action, a passion, or a cause, it takes the power of speech to convey the importance of said pursuits.

Lao Tzu, teaches: "From caring comes courage."

A vital element of bravery is being able to speak up when it is terrifying to do so. When was the last time you asked for help? When was the last time you said, "I'm a bit vulnerable at the moment, I need to figure out why?"

Bravery isn't always an outward display of character. Having the self-awareness to restrain oneself is an underexplored example of bravery. Bravery is not only about acting publicly or about speaking up, but about being silent when the times call for it. Not every situation requires our voice; not every pursuit needs our opinion. Knowing when to back off is as important, maybe even more so, than to stand up.

When we don't start from the masculine, ego-filled position to be a hero, but with the compassionate conviction of love, then we step back when we need to. To do this, we often need to rebuild trust and connectedness. The necessity of harnessing *the will to not act on our fear*, even at a moment when it might feel most appropriate.

So then, *What challenges or opportunities are present for me raising Charlie in a family where there is no mother, no significant female role model? What does it mean to be a 'father' in a time where the base identity of a 'male' is being challenged? Even called 'toxic'?*

I keep hearing if Charlie is a 'daddy's girl' or if 'she has me wrapped around her little finger' (which are both definitely the case), I may hinder her growth as an independent and self-sufficient individual. But bravery is cultivated and as an 'old school man's man'. Coming into this parenting thing found me lying awake at night worrying about not only the stuff I didn't know but also the stuff apparently, I'd been doing wrong. How does someone get to forty-nine without knowing you must NEVER wipe a butt in the wrong direction! This, believe it or not, is one of the most proffered pieces of advice offered by mums that was coming from a genuine place of love.

I absolutely loved (and still do) everything about being Charlie's dad right from the start. Her complete dependence on me filled me initially with fear and terror and I came face-to-face with my fallibility and flaws, and then a sense of purpose and achievement like nothing else. The night feeds, the nappy changes and bath time, having this amazing little miracle relying on me was the most masculine I'd ever felt.

In that time, I've cried more than I'd cried in the all the years of living. I struggle to hold in the tears every single time Charlie has a needle. I sat in the in the car and cried like a baby outside of Charlie's first day at kindergarten. I cried at Charlie's first ballet class, first gymnastics class; so many tear-stained firsts. Every single birthday still sees me incoherently trying not to embarrass her. Yet, I feel more masculine than ever. This is honest vulnerability.

Up until this point it had been all fun and games with no real parenting philosophy — just go with the flow and have fun spending every minute together. Almost every night for five years Charlie has crawled into my bed to elbow and kick me like some midget ninja. I remember being told she needs to sleep in her own bed. The night she moved into her own bedroom filled me with emotions of my little girl growing up too fast and the realisation that I can't stop time. Charlie noticed my usual inability to hold back my 'happy tears' and reassured me that she was only down the hall. Thankfully, the stoic independence did not last long and in the middle of the night she crawled into my bed with a wide selection of her favourite teddies which were fastidiously arranged before she snuggled into her favourite spot next to me draping her legs and arms over me like a drunk octopus.

Why does Charlie need to sleep in her own bed every night? How can I say to her (or more importantly show her) 'it doesn't matter when, where or what it is, if you need me, I'm there for you'? I'd hate to think of her hesitating to call me in the middle of the night when she's sixteen at a party. I want Charlie to know that the relationship we have cultivated is so strong that she has no issue picking up the phone for me to fetch her if she needs me to. I want her to have complete faith that no matter what situation or circumstance she finds herself in, I am only a call away.

I will never judge or desert. I will fetch, carry, listen and support her. There is no compromise; no 'I told you so'. I will be there the same way then, as when she climbed into my bed when she was a bub, battling to understand the gripping fear of the boogie man to when she is an adult and wanting reassurance in any way or form.

I understand that co-sleeping can divide parents – due to the safety and the developmental needs of children and the physical needs of the parents. It has even been suggested that sharing a bed with Charlie is inappropriate. It is just maddening. *Would the same inference be made if it were a son crawling in with his mother?*

I don't get a great night's sleep with her managing to take up ninety-six percent of the bed but being tired from being her dad is the most rewarding tired I've ever experienced. She has no concept of my personal space; always on my lap at movies, restaurants; even under the impression its 'our' dessert? At home this kid must be on top of me like a barnacle. Not sure why we even have a toilet door anymore.

"How will she cope if she has to be away from you?" I hear this often and yet Charlie's fearlessness is sometimes a little disconcerting for me. Charlie will try anything I challenge her to do showing no trepidation about going away from me. We are extremely lucky to have so many female friends in our life and Charlie relishes a girl's day out without me and enthusiastically goes for sleepovers whenever she can. I'm the one who struggles.

Charlie and I can't be too attached. It's our rock-solid attachment that allows Charlie to trust me — allows me to guide her. It is our unconditional relationship that frees Charlie from looking for love and allows her to grow. Charlie shouldn't have to work for love, not with me, and definitely not with any future partner. Charlie needs to see the example of love not being conditional on certain behaviours, compliance, or convenience.

There are two things Charlie should be when she grows up: WHO & WHAT she wants!

Being so much older than Charlie the reality is that she'll spend the majority of her life without me, so the ultimate goal is raising Charlie to become her own separate person. I want Charlie to have her own mind, set her own goals, come up with her own reasons, make her own decisions, think for herself, set her own boundaries.

Charlie feels certain her need for unconditional love will be met; she doesn't have to be preoccupied with pursuing me because she knows she can count on me as her dad, protector, and provider. She can count on me to guide and nurture her. Charlie doesn't need to cling to me.

Charlie used to cling to me as a preschooler out of insecurity. But it is her security in our attachment that frees Charlie and allows her to let go of me. Attachment isn't the enemy of growth, but insecure relationships will be both now, and in her adult life.

I realise only retrospectively that we have confirmed the studies about attachment theories. I never knew that an attachment was formed between a child and an individual by the time they hit the eighteen month mark, then it can be any caregiver that makes the child feel safe. I suppose you immediately just think that it would be the mum as she is the one that has direct contact with the bubs for the first few months. With our secure attachment well and truly formed, Charlie will hopefully know that she can rely on me for absolutely everything and anything.

> Rather than fatherhood being limiting as it may appear from the outside, I've found fatherhood has given me the freedom to cast off the ego, façade, and pretence and actually discover who I am as a person and as a man.

Don't get me wrong, I still need to be the disciplinarian, but just as importantly a nurturer. Never a feared figure but an example of respect and affection. The traditional gender roles in a relationship isn't something I'd necessarily want for Charlie's future relationships. Charlie needs to be convinced of her value and recognise when others don't.

I still need to be caring but firm. Charlie has to know she can depend on me if she's told her behaviour is not okay. I make sure she understands that the relationship still is. So, the idea of using what Charlie cares about against her, for example, sanctions and withdrawing privileges, or forms of separation-based discipline, such as time-outs just doesn't sit well with me. My love for Charlie is not contingent on a certain set of behaviours. I don't want Charlie to be preoccupied with whether her actions will cause me to love her more or less. She must count on my love regardless of her actions. I will encourage and support her values and that will hopefully grow her into a principled person. Don't get me wrong, there are certainly consequences to actions that are not acceptable. But love is a definite; a constant and firm pillar that will stand the test of time.

Most importantly, I realise that Charlie is always watching and what I do matters way more than what I say. I need to be asking myself what Charlie is learning about life in general, about morality, about how people should treat one another, about relationships from observing me every day.

An observation I have made while talking to a myriad of Dads is the irrevocable claim that they would do ANYTHING for their kids. Absolutely ANYTHING — pause for effect — except treat the kid's mums with respect purely because it is not reciprocal. Somehow, I find that love and the best interest of the kids has now become transactional or conditional.

My masculinity used to mean not being comfortable showing, or even admitting fear, but since girls tend to look to their mothers and immediate family for models of bravery, boys look to public figures, and as Charlie doesn't have her mother in her life, it's important that I share my fears with Charlie, as well as how I tackle those fears.

How is Charlie seeing me be brave? How is Charlie seeing me struggle? Seeing me fail?

Having Charlie see me fail and seeing me recover shows her how to be resourceful and resilient. I'm constantly and genuinely asking Charlie for help, input and opinions. She grows ten feet tall when I tell her we're a team! This kid loves to feel as though she's contributing to everything around the house.

> I think a lot of it is social constructs around expectations that are placed on us by others.

Charlie doesn't need a hero who's infallible, invincible, or stoic. I need to resist the urge to rescue, to remove obstacles, to pick her up when she gets knocked down. Charlie needs to build the mindset that failing, and recovering, is the natural order of things and the only way to true growth, over and over again, so she believes she can do it herself.

I can't rob Charlie of the 'gift' of failure. Failing at the small things, especially while she is young, will allow her to develop the resilience and confidence she needs to tackle larger issues. We must keep one eye on the task at hand, but the vision firmly on her life ahead.

I'm unable to speak through experience about what it means to be a woman or the myriad of things that go with that. So, it's important that Charlie's feelings are never dismissed as trivial. As her dad, I don't need to understand. I just need to know it's important to her.

It's down to me to guide Charlie through milestones like puberty, menstruation and romantic interests. Apparently, I'll be expected to eat ice cream with Charlie straight from the tub after failed relationships? Don't need to understand it, I just need to support her.

These things as a male will be difficult without Charlie trusting me. It will be about me learning with her although that's exactly what we've done together as a team from day one.

This kid has taught me just as much as I have her. When you realise your kid wants to be exactly like you — when you realise she looks to you for how to respond to life and its challenges, what to value and what to dismiss; looks to you for the example of love, honesty and empathy — you do better.

When you realise you are her example of how someone who loves and respects her should treat her, you realise you need to support and nurture who she really is and not try to control or create who you think she should be because the thought of anyone controlling this kid breaks my heart — you do better.

When you realise getting a surprise bunch of flowers makes your daughters day. When you realise you might be the standard she accepts from future partners — you do better.

When you realise the way you speak to her will become her inner voice, her self-esteem, her confidence is all down to you. The way she perceives herself and others will be a reflection of the values you display, the way you react and even the lunchbox notes you write — you do better.

So, you might call Charlie a 'daddy's girl', you might say, 'Charlie has me wrapped around her little finger.' It doesn't really matter. No amount of distance, time or disagreements will ever break this team apart. Our bond couldn't be better.

Do I have all the answers? Definitely not, and I'm more than okay with that because together Charlie and I will keep searching for our truths, and this leads us to the event that changed our lives forever.

WHO KNEW?

Chapter Three

Only a Mother's Love?

"When society regularly talks about fatherhood in the same glowing terms as motherhood an inertia will be broken. When men are recognised and admired for their nurturing and raising of the next generation instead of their income, position or power, a paradigm will finally shift.

When men are held equally responsible for raising the next generation, women will achieve true equality, not only in the workplace, but in society in general. It's time to move from outdated gender and societal roles that are limiting ALL of us."

Michael Ray

When I refer to being the 'best parent' please don't misinterpret this as some Instagramable worthy aspiration. What I mean is that it doesn't matter to me what I achieve or accumulate in life but if I fail as a parent, then I am nothing but a failure.

I always tell Charlie that obstacles are always opportunities for growth. Your situation and circumstance are where innovation and adaptation thrive because of those constraints. The exposure to appropriate and meaningful struggle and stress is the catalyst from which strength, resilience and fulfillment are borne.

The clarity through crisis for me was real. After the initial diagnosis when I collided with the unfortunate tree that early morning and the subsequent treatments, the separation, and the lack of time I had with Charlie cleared the fog of indecision. Like a ray of sunshine, the thought of my daughter not growing up with me to have tea parties with, to paint nails and do hair, to not go on adventures with or lie on the couch together watching cartoons scared me, scared me to the bone. It made me realise that I had the power to make the changes in my life that would allow me to be able to create these memories. Being in the fitness industry I was able to manipulate my time to ensure that I was with Charlie on all the days that she was not at kindergarten. I would be there at her waking and be there to put her to bed. Yes, I did have to decide to forego the expensive car, the overseas holidays, the suppers out and the lavish shopping. Some call it luck that I was able to structure my life. I call it a conscious decision to spend my time with my daughter. It was never a hard decision; it was the only decision.

Hard isn't a fact, it's an attitude and attitude is vital.

Since Charlie was born, I see a baby and all of a sudden I'm making that high pitched 'AWWW' with no control, completely subconsciously but definitely audibly as evidenced by the smiles of the mothers.

'Only a Mother's love, maternal instinct, mother-knows-best' and all of the other fetishized depictions of motherhood that we've all heard a million times, read on everything from baby food to nappies, laundry powder to prams. Don't even get me started on the greeting cards that can still bring me to tears like a kid who's just dropped their ice cream in the middle of Kmart.

Airline commercials, toilet paper ads and even telco commercials depicting a call home at Christmas and I'm a blubbering mess. All cynical ploys to influence my spending but since Charlie has come into this world I've suddenly got no control over my emotions even though I know I'm being played. I've become emotionally incontinent!

And then there is kid's fashion! I can tell you exactly which shop, season and size any little girl is wearing. To go out with Charlie in matching outfits right down to matching nails we both feel like princesses.

Until Charlie was born, I had no idea that a love so intense could ever exist. An all-consuming overwhelming mix of fear of the unknown, a sense of such intense pride that it sometimes makes my heart feel like it's going to explode. I still remember the exact moment my life changed forever for the better. It's almost as though my life before was of no real consequence or significance just all-in preparation.

It's funny, isn't it? That the idea of a father having parenting instincts is as foreign as clean feet on a greedy pig. We have been so preconditioned to take on the role as breadwinner and provider or a poor assistant to a mother or merely the second adult in the room, that when we are seen with a child during the week, most will instinctively wonder where the mother is and comment on our 'babysitting' abilities.

Only a Mother's Love?

I can't tell you how many times in the last nine years since Charlie and I have been on our own that I've been asked, "How do you manage?" My answer is usually, "like any solo parent – just barely," until the follow up is, "No, sorry. I meant as a male trying to raise a daughter on his own?" I can't tell you how many times I've been told, "every little girl needs her mum."

The constant self-doubt if I'm doing things right, if I'm raising a secure, happy, confident little girl who isn't going to be on the news one day for torturing small animals. After a lifetime of hearing about, 'Only a Mother's Love', I'm filled with doubt if I'm good enough, doing enough, because the majority of the time I'm second guessing myself.

The worry if Charlie will be accepted and make friends even though we're a single parent family. The Dad guilt that I have to endure when Charlie asks me for a sleep over and I have to try and explain to her and her innocent brain that some parents may not want the little girls sleeping over at a man's house without a woman present. How do I tell her about societies preconceived notion of males being inherently evil and their apparent genetic want to harm and hurt?

I then think, will the mums notice how awkward I feel at gymnastics when I sit down as a fellow parent? Will they see how intimidated I am? I have walked into the hardest gyms and clubs in the world and been in the most precarious situations and still never felt the intimidation that I have felt when being confronted with a whole gaggle of mums.

Will I be able to make suitable small talk at school pick up with the other mums? It is funny, there is probably about one other dad that does the school pickup and like a little blessing of unicorns we have gravitated together purely out of necessity and fear.

It brings back memories of my school years where the cool kids would be off jabbering away and all of the 'other' kids were left on the outskirts dearly hoping that they would get the nod of approval and be included in the inner circle.

Will my lack of any real knowledge of what I'm doing raising this tiny human be that obvious that I'll be chased out of town by a laughing mob of 'real mothers?'

Only a Mother's Love?

Night feeds, nappy changes and bath time. I've loved every moment with Charlie. Still, to this day, there are nights where I'll sit on the edge of her bed and watch her sleeping bringing myself to tears with emotion and wondering how I could have been responsible for creating such a perfect little person.

Crawling, walking, teaching her to swim and ride a bike as a single parent, my confidence to not completely ruin this child grows.

Trips to the hospital sleeping in the chair watching over her, all survived. Trying my best to hide my tears as Charlie gets a needle (still, need to work on that). Charlie's fine, me not so much!

Suddenly people comment on her good manners and how happy and confident she is. Parent-teacher interviews and even report cards start to confirm I might actually not be stuffing up the most important thing I've ever taken on in my life?

> We support and encourage each other with advice from our own trials and tribulations of this messy and magical, exhausting and rewarding, exhilarating and sometimes terrifying thing called fatherhood.

Conversations through the toilet door, lunchbox notes and making costumes for Charlie's teddies on my sewing machine. *Only a mother's love, right?* In summary, Dads are simply no different – Who knew? Just as women can hold a position in a C-suite so dads can nurture their children. That overwhelming feeling when I held Charlie for the first time transcends any feeling I have experienced before.

The need to talk about her non-stop, to share her every twitch, her fart-smile, her little pursed lips and sucky-face she would pull when she was hungry!

I've read studies explaining that there is an alteration in the male hormones when they are presented with their little humans for the first time and their testosterone levels drop, they are less likely to take risks and their oxytocin increases — that is the 'feel-good' hormone.

Honestly, I don't need research to tell me that this overriding feeling of euphoria, empathy and absolute love is pure and real. It doesn't change anything I've written but hopefully, you'll see how 'mother's love' should be replaced with 'parents love'.

In a world where it's so politically correct and even a policeman is now a police person and a policewoman is also a police person, *how does this sexist last generation rubbish still exist?*

All of it is unacceptable and all of it is counterproductive to women who are rightfully arguing for equal pay and equal opportunity in today's society. Women, nor men, should not be held back by outdated gender stereotypes.

Women shouldn't be made to feel that their children are getting second best because the father is the primary caregiver. Men need to step up and be supported in their desire to be more connected and more respected for what they contribute to our children's lives.

> **My overriding advice is to get involved. Your children are only young once. It's the most magical time I've ever experienced, and it really isn't that hard – don't let the experts tell you otherwise.**

I'm not unusual.

I'm not special.

I'm a parent who just happens to be a dad and once you're a parent it's not about you anymore. Its ALL about your children. I'm not babysitting. I'm parenting. It's not even what I'm doing; its who I am now.

I don't sacrifice anything for Charlie because there's nothing I'd rather be doing; my life is better every minute of every day because Charlie gives meaning and purpose to everything I do. Charlie is raising me rather than the other way around. She's always watching everything so I have to be the example of who she should be and how she should be treated.

The good news is that slowly things are changing. Advertisers are starting to use fathers in supermarket ads. Support groups for dads are popping up which is all very encouraging but as parents we ALL need to support and respect the amazing role we play as caregivers and role models irrespective of our gender family make up.

But you know, if Charlie's mum and I hadn't separated, I probably would have slept-walked into the typical gendered role of me being the breadwinner. And assuming that being a good dad meant providing and protecting and that I would judge my success as a father on my ability to provide for my family. Whereas now, I realised that this ideology is not the best. Coming from a unique position of being surrounded by mums, sometimes, like a fly on the wall, I have a completely different perspective.

A lot of the mum-guilt and mum-shame is the exact same for dads; off killing themselves and feeling terrible and dissatisfied with working when they'd rather be home with little Johnny who's got sport, or a school play; but I'm here at work, feeling like I'm letting him down, locked into this breadwinner role.

And a lot of the times mums feel like, "you know, I'd actually like some outside stimulation," or "I want to use my career. I studied all those years," and "I would like some of this," and they feel bad because, "my children, they come first."

> When society talks about fatherhood in the same glowing terms as motherhood, inertia will be broken. When men are recognised and admired for their nurturing and raising of the next generation instead of their income, position or power, a paradigm will finally shift.
>
> When men are held equally responsible for raising the next generation, women will achieve true equality, not only in the workplace, but society in general.

Parenting is a learned skill.

The term 'maternal instinct' or phrases such as 'Only a Mothers Love' should be thrown in the rubbish bin of history and replaced with 'parental instinct' and 'only a parents love,' otherwise we are placing more pressure, obligation and responsibilities onto women.

The archaic belief behind maternal instinct is that women are better equipped both psychologically and physiologically for parenting. Please don't think I am some 'woke new-age, enlightened bloke'. I think a lot of social constructs around expectations are placed on us, by others.

I grew up in a very traditional household. Mum and dad had a typical marriage in that dad was the breadwinner. Mum ran the house. Mum didn't even have a driver's licence until dad had a stroke later on in life because dad did everything for mum outside of the home. When people say to me, "it's great that you're embracing the role of mum and dad," I reply, "No, I have embraced the role of a parent."

Some of us are good parents because of our parents. Some of us are good parents, despite our parents. I am definitely a product of my parents. There are often times when I hear my mother coming out of my mouth at random intervals like some possessed character that has been taken over by my mother's parenting spirit. Without thinking I hear myself repeating phrases from my childhood, *"elbows off the table*," *"I wasn't born yesterday, you know." "You will live,"* and even a well-worn and precautionary, *"I can see this ending in tears."* As a father I seem to be doing an awfully good impression of my mother.

For all intents and purposes, I am not a father fathering or a father mothering, I am a parent, parenting.

Growing up, I can honestly not remember a single father household, while I am sure that they existed. The future I imagined for myself was pretty much a carbon copy of what my mum and dad had. If my life was going to involve children it was most certainly going to involve a mother and follow the standard nuclear family blueprint. A future with a mother wrangling and attending to the children and me as her faithful and trusty sidekick and ace assistant. I also imagined the future to have flying cars and hover boards thanks to a well-known cult film. Looks like I was wrong on all counts – Who knew?

Currently, as I write this, the fastest growing family demographic in Australia is single father households estimated to increase between 40 - 65% by the 2041 census. At present 1 in 5 single parent households are fathers. Stay at home fathers in a two-parent household increased from 60,000 in 2008 to over 80,000 in 2011. While the percentage of dads remains relatively small at 4% of stay-at-home parents, it represents a fascinating shift in gender expectations that needs to be considered and facilitated to advance gender equality.

The challenge I face, is that I am generally seen as unusual or odd. This does not refer in any way to my unique fashion-sense or my enthusiastic dance moves to outdated 70's disco tunes, or chicken dance at every opportunity which usually is at the pre-school bell much to Charlie's embarrassment. This seems to refer to people's perceptions of our family situation. It is uncommon given the figure quoted but it happens repeated and regularly. So, while it is uncommon, *why do we see it as unusual?*

Many of our equality initiatives seek to apply an equitable outcome to an unequal beginning, we are basically parking the ambulance at the bottom of the cliff-treating the symptoms rather than the cause. Often the unintended consequence is easing the symptoms just enough to enable the status quo to continue with women responsible for raising the next generation.

True equality must begin in the home and the workplace will have to accommodate the workforce instead of the current tail wagging the dog. What we exemplify in the home and what our children see from our example, will be their expectations. From my upbringing, I assumed that being a good dad meant being the provider, protector and disciplinarian, with the additional title of Recreational and Amusement Co-Ordinator and Distractor in Chief, freeing Mum up to do even

MORE mum stuff or heaven forbid 'catch her breath' and put her feet up at the end of the day.

> If your behaviour is governed or influenced by what is typical, expected or popular, rather than what is required for your family, ethical and authentic, you don't have a problem with your masculinity. You have a problem with your character.

It was on these strict KPI's that I would judge my success as a father. Given that my example was a hetro-normative nuclear family, my challenge was to fulfil both roles. The solution was to decide what was most important and what trade-offs I was prepared to make.

We constantly hear about the sacrifices that parents make for their children. I remember thinking how much my parents sacrificed for us kids for our family. As I see it now, sacrifice is giving up something of great value for something of lesser value. I prefer the term 'trade-offs.' There are many trade-offs I've made as a Dad and I would make every one of them willingly again because they are pretty good deals.

There is nothing that happens outside of the home that is not made instantly better by the enthusiastic and joyful cry of 'Dad!' when we reunite at the end of the day.

With Mums erringly annoying and prophetic wisdom ringing in my ears, I could hear another one of her well-worn phrases, "If everyone was jumping off a cliff, would you?" I was forced to consider if the stereotypical representation and expectation, not only of fatherhood, but also of success was a cliff that I was prepared to jump off. There are numerous studies on father's income levels and children's outcomes, as far as emotional, social, even physical well-being go.

The clear message from the research is, with the exception of the 20% of children living in poverty, income is not consistently linked to better psychological, behavioural, emotional outcomes or the quality of the relationships with their parents. Time spent with parents, connection, and the bond between the parents and the child has a larger impact.

Several questions arise from this –

- *If you were to sacrifice some of your income for more time spent with your children, would your children be better off?*
- *How much of my work is simply providing for my children and how much do I find identity, satisfaction, and fulfilment from it?*

There is nothing wrong with that. But don't kid yourself that you're doing it for the kids. And don't kid yourself saying, "I've got to work to be a good dad."

- *What sort of dad do you want to be remembered as?*
- *What do you want your children to tell their children about you?*

At forty-nine I never thought I would have children. At fifty-eight I never thought I would be approached to write a book and I definitely never thought or even dreamed that I would one day be quoting Pope John xxii, but when the man is right, the man is right! So here goes ...

It is easier for a father to have children

than for children to have a real father.

— *Pope John XXII*

JUST BE THAT DAD

For me good parenting is the ability to turn the ordinary into the extraordinary. What I mean by this is turning the ordinary mundane into extraordinary memorable events.

'Good enough' parenting is just that; 'Good Enough'.

I remember the look of shock and delight on Charlie's face when I wondered into the bathroom one night while she was head deep in bubble bath bubbles. I tottered in balancing the dinner dishes on both arms like a well-seasoned waiter and loudly announced that she was now old enough to help with the cleaning up after dinner.

She sat quietly for a moment, not completely sure what to say or how to react. She eventually said, "Okay dad, but why do you have the dishes with you?" I answered, "Well, I thought since that we are always pressed for time these days we may as well multi-task." I'm told that men are unable to do this. Well, did I prove them wrong!

PLOP! PLOP! PLOP! went each plate, knife and fork, and coffee cup, into the bath!

I have never in my fifty-eight years on this planet seen a child tackle the tedious chore of washing dishes with such gusto! Never did I see little arms swish and sway to flurry up even more bubbles until I could barely even see her.

With each dish cleaned she would proudly lift the dish above her head to see the glint of light to confirm the shine and sparkle that can only be achieved with bubbles. I think she told everyone she spoke to over the next couple of weeks about our laughter-filled bath time.

Was she bathed perfectly? Did the dishes need to be rewashed after she was in bed? Of course, however for me, it was about creating the memory and absolutely nothing to do with quality control — good enough, was good enough.

> "When fathers perceive their children to be capable of a task, it is linked not only with the children's positive perceptions of their own abilities, but also with the degree to which they value the task."
>
> (Bhanot & Jovanovic, 2009).

Sometimes I do get so busy in the day-to-day stuff that I lose sight of how special it is to be a dad. I remind myself that it's all about that connection.

With the prevalence of social media in all forms we seem to be inundated with perfection; the perfect life, the perfect job, the perfect smile. The constant need for likes and comments becomes almost an obsession. The fear that I have for my daughter is real. The unrealistic expectation that this sets for her and the high level of credence that is placed on getting this recognition is built on very shaky ground.

I have become a living embodiment of Facebook and Instagram where she was just seeing everything that was right and perfect and I have to admit the opportunity to appear as a superhero to my daughter is very intoxicating. After all, who doesn't want to be their child's superhero to swoop in at any minute and keep them safe and secure.

But in a moment of frustration and doubt of her ability, maybe even her self-worth, words came out, "Dad I wish I could do everything as good as you." Had I been trying to show off? *Was I being a peacock – show boating, trying to gain the lofty admiration of an eight-year-old and not letting her see the doubt, the fear, the struggles, that are a natural part of life?*

As dads we are heroic and larger than life in every way. I know my dad was to me and it is only now that I am older that I realise how much went into all of his achievements. I understand while he could do anything, he took the time to teach me how to do it for myself. While he didn't make it past grade six he encouraged me and insisted I persevere at school. My dad didn't just build a house; he built a home for his family. He didn't just build successful businesses; he provided for his family and it wasn't my father's hands that did this – it was his heart and soul.

Charlie's birthday last year was once again another incredible learning event for me. You will note my life is peppered with my daughter teaching me the simple facts of life in the most bizarre and palm slapping ways. Charlie wanted to bake a cake for her birthday. She was quiet adamant that she wanted a fox, the latest animal in the line of favourites. We spent many a night scouring the internet finding the perfect recipe. As she excitedly proclaimed, "Dad, how about this one? No. No. This one." My heart started to sink; with every passing picture the foxes became more elaborate.

Never one to shy away from a challenge, we eventually agreed on the beast that was to be produced together in our humble kitchen. After the decision was made and a very excited seven-year-old had showed nanny and called her aunt and cemented the cake baking sentence into a reality.

As we lay in bed that night ruminating and doing imaginary purchasing of all of the ingredients and fine-tuning the fox to her specifications, I said, "Bubs, this may not turn out as good as the picture." To this she replied, "That's okay Dad, didn't you say that you just have to give it your best? We will do it together anyway."

I welled up – as was now to be expected. The realisation that the values that I wrote of earlier shone through the innocence and love of my most prized possession. We were amped to get this cake baked.

I tackled the cake baking as I have fatherhood; not as some woke, educated, or researched baker, but as a fun adventure to create yet another experience that I would be able to play on the spools of memory when she finally decided that I was no longer interesting or entertaining – except my fabulous dad jokes, she will always love those!

The day finally arrived and Charlie walked into the kitchen looking like she was going to defuse a bomb. I stopped in my tracks and asked her why this attire was required for cake baking. She looked at me with those piercing blue eyes, dancing with delight and excitement. "Dad, did you not say that it may not turn out as good? I think it's only wise that we are prepared for anything."

WHO KNEW?

Chapter Four

The Only Unicorn in the Village

"The best aspect of being a Dad would be the chance to once again view the world vicariously through the eyes of a child. Everything is amazing and exciting, new, and untainted by expectations or experience. The ability to be completely present in the moment is the elixir of life for me."

Michael Ray

I couldn't be more amazed at the little dweeb that I'm now the example to. I am also aware, thanks to viewing the world from Charlie's perspective, that we are striving to make gains in gender equality, not only in the workplace but also in society. Hopefully, if Charlie becomes a mum one day, instead of rigid roles, parenthood by then should provide men and women with a space to explore themselves, as it has done for me as a sole parent.

Charlie is growing up in a time and place where she has full control over her reproductive rights, can marry her partner regardless of their gender, be another female Prime Minister and most importantly to me, even be a professional AFL footballer (as long as she plays for Essendon that is).

> The latest census shows almost 1 in 5 single parent households are now fathers. Almost 1 in 4 stay at home parents are now fathers.

Charlie should be able to achieve all of this without the first question being asked, "How will you manage this with a family?" This is not something that high-achieving men are ever asked.

We've always heard about amazing single mother's and the sacrifices and successes they have raising their kids. *Why then, at the age of fifty-six, did I suddenly wonder if I was the only Unicorn in the village?*

When I hear the term 'I sacrifice everything for my kids' it makes me a bit sad. When I look at Charlie, nothing is a sacrifice. Sacrifice to me denotes regret, loss, or compromise. When we speak of parenthood it is a noble and scary role. We place ourselves on a pedestal and profess all that we do to provide, nurture and protect our young. *Is this simply not parenthood?*

I chose to be single not because I was sacrificing my life for Charlie but because I did not want a partner to feel that they were not a priority. Charlie and I am a choice, a choice that I am happy with.

As an adult when someone says that they have sacrificed something for you, I want you to think about how that makes you feel as a fully-formed and functioning human and see the negative and culpable emotions it evokes. Now try and transfer that to a child that is not intellectually or emotionally equipped to understand the phrase. Can you imagine thinking how they are that much of a burden that it is due to them that they have to work as hard, work two jobs, or whatever you perceive you sacrifice.

What changed my perspective and made me feel like I was the only Unicorn in the village?

It started with simple playground visits – outings that we regularly enjoyed. As a first-time nervous dad with absolutely no idea of what I was doing these outings were planned like a well-oiled black ops field trip and the baggage resembled that of a World War I field hospital. I know there is lot of head nodding in agreement. We have all seen 'that' parent.

I would pack into an all-terrain pram that was obviously designed and built to enable high speed running, that cost more than the car I drove, enough organic, U-beaut baby food to sustain us for 3 days (all packed with freezer blocks in a Hi-Tec, NASA certified cooler bag), plus various 'superfood', Paleo, sugar free snack options in case an impromptu tasting platter was more suitable for bubs. Plus, enough water, hand sanitiser, sterile wipes and various first aid accessories to survive any wild animal attack, insect, spider or venomous snake bite or even the sudden onset of Ebola. Add to that, approximately seventeen nappies, three complete changes of colour coordinated, cute as could be outfits, all suitable and necessary for any variation in UV index, temperature, climate, or worst of all, a misaligned, defective or simply overflowing nappy!

The one issue that we did have however, was that of simple logistics – NO CHANGE TABLES in the men's toilets at a park. Apparently, men don't take toddlers to the park. *Have I not read the 'training toddlers to only fill a nappy at home' section of some manual that other dads had?*

> We have syringe disposals in men's toilets but not change tables. Are men more likely to be drug users than fathers?

This meant that I would have to take my chances on a blanket under a tree (weather permitting), or balancing a squirming, faecally challenged infant on my lap like some daring circus juggler, or in the boot of my car — much to the misfortune of passing spectators that would witness the final destination of the mashed vegetables, teething husks and a variety of unidentified food scraps from the floor that Charlie had somehow managed to beat the dog to.

On one such occasion, some wonderful ladies suggested I should be changing Charlie in the male toilets on the change tables provided for just such an occasion. The funny thing was, the 'considerate' ladies made me realise there *ARE* change tables in the women's toilets but *NOT* the men. This made me wonder, *are men more likely to be drug users than fathers? Do dad's not take their kids to the park? Or is changing a nappy simply women's work? Could it be I'm the only Unicorn in the village?*

While on one of these excursions I, being a doting dad with the stealth like ability of a David Attenborough wildlife cameraman, was snapping photos of my baby girl in the natural habitat of the child; the playground, when a very disgruntled woman stormed over and demanded to know why I was taking photos of 'the child'. The look on her face when I informed her that she was actually MINE… LOL! Apparently, I AM the only Unicorn in the village.

Numerous times Charlie and I casually ventured into the parent's room only to be asked why we were there because apparently, a Unicorn makes it difficult for 'real' parents to breastfeed. *Who knew?*

Are there some secretive rituals being performed in a parent's room that dads have not been suitably licenced, certified, and registered with the correct agency to be part of? Maybe I am the only Unicorn in the village.

Aren't I simply a parent? Surely no more or no less than any other parent? We've removed the gendered terms from so many areas in our modern world. We now have Police **Person**, Chair **Person**,

Fire *Person* and titles such as Male Nurse are long gone, and the list goes on.

Yet we still have offensive terms such as 'Deadbeat Dad' instead of 'Deadbeat *Parent*' where the proportion of mothers saying no child support was paid was about the same whether they were payees or payers which was 12% and 13% respectively. However, the proportion of fathers saying nothing was paid was much higher when they were payees rather than payers which was 21% and 2% respectively. To be fair though, mothers' more consistent reports may indicate greater accuracy compared with fathers.

Finally, with the constant issue of Charlie's nappies and the lack of change tables behind us (and the issue of incontinence nappies for me starting to loom large with my advancing years), things would get easier as we rushed towards milestones such as loosing teeth – probably both of us – riding a bike, starting school. All well within the realm of a mere male masquerading as a parent.

These gender stereotypes start early due to societal norms. The generalisations oversimplifying the expected roles hold us all back. I used to love taking Charlie along to ballet class on a Tuesday morning. There is nothing cuter than a gaggle of tiny ballerinas all decked out in in their dance gear; hair pulled tight into a ballet bun, except me in my ballet kit.

Now don't get me wrong, I love a compliment as much as anyone. Actually, probably more truth be told, and did the compliments come thick and fast. "So good to see a dad here with his daughter." "Who does her bun? It's perfect!" (Thank goodness for YouTube tutorials) "She's so lucky to have you," even proudly being considered an honorary mum – 'one of the girls'.

Frankly, we men should find it patronising to be praised so highly for accomplishing everyday parenting tasks, so let's just calm down about dads doing normal stuff with their kids. If we keep making routine acts of fatherhood such a huge deal, boys will never learn that this bottle-making, baby-wearing, ponytail-creating level of fatherhood isn't superhuman. It's what's expected of them.

However, after a while some of the questions and comments made me wonder — Don't you work? Where is her mum? How do you manage? Don't you think little girls need their mums? Who picked out that beautiful outfit? Even, what will you do when Charlie reaches puberty?

I could never imagine asking these questions to a mum. *Could I be that much of an oddity?* Aren't I simply a parent? There is that only Unicorn in village again.

Charlie and I did a bit of an informal research project after she pointed out while shopping one day that there were very few men on any of the packaging for cleaning or childcare products. I would like to think that she noticed this due to our unique family setup. Watching Charlie adapt to the world, she seeks out explanations from her environment and I have watched while this has shaped her perception of what is 'normal' for others and how she reacts and interprets this information. Because she has grown up in what is deemed an unconventional family, I feel that the stereotypical representations have been challenged.

After Charlie mentioned this to me we decided to go and do some day time investigation. So, armed with the mobile phone and a note pad we dropped in at a number of big supermarket stores and trawled the isles, noting products of all types and looked carefully at the packaging. The general consensus as noted by Charlie is that women did the cleaning of the house except for polishing furniture and cleaning the oven. We noted that according to the packaging on most baby products, childcare was a women's job. It's a subtle reminder that the subliminal advertising grooms and prepares women and men for the outdated gender stereotypical division of work in the home.

Trying to find children's books or nursery rhymes with a father as the primary caregiver or anything other than a disciplinarian, or a hero coming to save some poor damsel in distress was virtually impossible. I'm used to editing on the fly, substituting mum for dad often ruining any rhyming in the process for anyone not as adept as Dr. Seuss. There is research out that a child is 1.6 times more likely to read a book with a male lead and seven times more likely to read a book with a male villain. Not only are these statistics staggering but it has been found that father characters are grossly underrepresented.

We now create our own stories and have shelved all the traditional story books. We now have a band of unlikely animals that form an eclectic family and travel the world saving all the lonely, lost and injured animals and make them family. I think we are now sitting on about twenty-three fur-family members – my aged mind is battling to remember all of them as they ALL need a mention every night! I do need to point out that we have approximately seventeen real, live pets and I have to remember their names too.

Overall, 'father love' appears to be as heavily implicated as 'mother love' in their offspring's psychological wellbeing and health, as well as in an array of behavioural problems. Children with involved, caring fathers also have better educational outcomes. The influence of a father's involvement extends into adolescence and young adulthood. Numerous studies suggest that an active and nurturing style of fathering is associated with better verbal skills, intellectual functioning, and academic achievement among adolescents. So why do less than 5% of fathers take the full amount of paternity leave available to them? To achieve gender equality both in the workplace and the home, it is essential for men to have an equal chance to be there with their newborn babies.

Numerous studies have found that fathers taking parental leave not only help close the wage gap and increases participation in unpaid household duties by up to 250% but also helps men form long-term bonds with their children. Extending a father's leave to one month or more tends to make men more assertive in parenting rather than deferring to mothers. Fathers on extended leave do more housework, and savour time spent with their infants more.

Individual entitlement to parental leave for fathers clearly provides a framework for encouraging men's assumption of full responsibility for the care of children. This is a vital step in equality for women, not only in the workplace but in general.

In my travels, speaking to fathers who want to become more actively involved in their children's lives, they often hit barriers such as I've experienced from employers, the media, and even their wives, who may feel threatened by a child calling for 'Daddy' instead of 'Mummy'.

> The only way women will achieve true equality in the workplace and elsewhere, is when men are held equally responsible for raising the next generation.

A noted sociologist, Dr. David Popenoe, is one of the pioneers of the relatively young field of research into fathers and fatherhood. "Fathers are far more than just 'second adults' in the home," he says. "Involved fathers bring positive benefits to their children that no other person is as likely to bring. Fathers have a direct impact on the well-being of their children."

Just doing whatever your partner tells you is still leaving responsibilities to her. The whole attitude of 'helping' with the kids makes fathers an assistant, not an accomplished, capable parent.

Becoming a sole parent has made me a better father and an example of what Charlie should expect from a partner as it forced me to step forward and take responsibility for dealing with situations that in the past I probably would have just left for my partner to handle or to tell me what to do.

Gender inequity is structural and systemic. It affects both women and men. It's not only about the jobs we hold but it's also about cultural expectations and assumptions about family values. Today, the workplace and family are all in transition, yet most of our social norms were established in a bygone time. Ultimately, it is unrealistic to expect one part of our lives to change without completely disrupting the others. If Charlie is really going to break through all the glass ceilings, we'll also need to let go of the incompetent dad stigma.

Dads, I love you all, but I'm not falling all over myself because you acted like a *parent*. We're capable. We're intelligent. We're great at it. We play a crucial role particularly in the cognitive, behavioural, and general health and well-being areas of a child's life. We are the example for our children, and we should be doing it all the damn time.

WHO KNEW?

Chapter Five

Love simply is "The quality of attention we give to others."

"It is the moment between the moments, where the magic often is. Those seemingly nothing moments that can become the glue that cements the childhood memories and connections in place.

Those memories will be a rock-solid anchor in trying times - a template, a standard, and the medium in which we've planted the seeds of the garden from where
their lives will grow!"

Michael Ray

Love, simply is, 'The Quality of Attention We Give to Others.'

We all have competing demands in today's hectic life, but the one thing that is within our control is the quality, if not the quantity, of the time we have with our children.

When we place a premium on the scarcity of any resource its value naturally increases. For those that think that is just too wordy let me try to make it really simple; every day there are amazing moments with your children. Pay attention or you will miss them. This is where we can make the biggest impact, have the biggest influence, and ensure the biggest connection that will form fond, firm and lasting memories for them to carry with them through life.

I want Charlie to question most things in her life EXCEPT her importance, self-worth, or my love.

As parents we all wonder and all doubt ourselves. We question if we are enough, doing enough, and being enough. These insecurities add to an already stressful life of social, school and sport commitments, along with the usual daily work grind and stresses. The ones that make your left eye twitch and makes you want to find a quiet secluded spot for your head to stop pounding and to just be still for a moment. But then there is supper to cook, dishes to wash, shopping to do, house to clean, homework to supervise and the dog needs a walk.

I went into fatherhood without the curse of knowledge; without any expectations and without any societal KPI's. Fatherhood has been nothing but fun for me and fortunately I've got the easiest kid in the world. There was no parenting brilliance, no special skills, no secret sauce, just pure luck. Since I have started studying Developmental

Psychology, retrospectively I have noted that we had hit all the required milestones and variations in development that are considered usual without any of the pressure, worry, or expectations because I was a blissful, know nothing parent.

At a recent talk I had a parent ask me what my coping mechanisms were when it comes to dividing my time and balancing a career and being a solo dad.

My response, my mantra, my belief is, 'The Quality of Your Attention Is Love'. Especially important for those parents possibly distant from the daily contact with their children for whatever reason.

So, I have five opportunities each day where I aim to really focus my attention for the greatest impact with Charlie.

1. ***Before School:*** The absolute worst way to set the tone for the day is with a stressful, mad rush to get out the door. Again, and as I have said before — routine, routine, routine. We make an effort at removing the rush by preparing as much of the morning's routine the previous evening. Charlie is included in this by making her own lunch, laying out her uniform and packing her school bag, while I wash the dinner dishes. She loves to feel that she is contributing to the family and she embraces the responsibility.

   We make it a mission to sit in the front veranda regardless of the weather and feed the magpies that throng our garden. We sit and jabber about nothing and everything.

There are days when we are ill-prepared for the day and the house resembles a scene from Die Hard. There is wrestling with school socks and the throwing of lunch boxes and school shoes across the living room. The laughter is loud, the stress is real, and the outcome is sometimes questionable, but we make it through, and we live to have another morning and know that we need to ensure that we keep to routine and prepare everything at night.

2. *After School*: Nothing beats long summer days in Melbourne and in the Ray family this means unscheduled adventures to the swimming pool after school. It turns into who can make the biggest water bomb, see who can dive off the highest diving board or how high I can shoot her in the air before she pirouettes into a back flip. Then its ice-cream and home for fish and chips in the beach tent in front of TV. Some afternoons just drawing on the driveway with Charlie or sitting on the veranda and once again just chilling and chatting. I know not everyone has the ability to be able to schedule their lives to have this time available and that is why I write that these are times that I have made available. They are not always a given as I have work commitments but when I do there is no guilty pleasure but rather a languish in the decedent time together.

3. *Dinner Time*: It is family tradition to have dinner at the table, except of course on special occasions. Charlie absolutely loves helping me cook, and it takes forever. I sometimes feel that there should be another word for HELP when the help is provided by an eight-year-old. Sometimes it is most definitely

the opposite of help. But it is her intention that is appreciated and even better is her sense of having contributed to our dinner that is my reward.

Routine, routine, routine, routine — children thrive on routine. Children find great comfort knowing exactly what is expected from them and still being given the autonomy to get it done. This is the cornerstone or the rock-solid foundation for successful parenting, known as authoritative parenting.

4. **Bedtime**: This is why I feel that bedtime is so important. We discuss the day; the good, the bad and the confusing. I feel that this time that we have carved out together is the perfect platform for her to feel safe and happy to discuss any issues that she has. We discuss everything from friends made and lost, work done in the classroom, things that happened in the playground. There is no topic undiscussed. We finish the night with her gratitude journal, which always has animals featured in some way or form. This is also the time as stated in the previous chapter when we tell our elaborate made-up story with the million animals and my weary old brain has to remember all the characters, back-stories, and come up with exciting new adventures. It is no wonder that I fall asleep before Charlie does.

I can't count the number of nights as I wonder through the house bleary eyed on the way to bed picking all of the discarded and misplaced items from clothing to toys, switching off enough lights to illuminate the dark side of the moon and adjusting the thermostat, as every dad is genetically and biologically programmed to do.

Too many nights, as this process winds its way down the hall, I stop at Charlie's room to deposit the armful of stuff with a mental note to remind her in the morning of her obligation to tidy her own stuff, a quick adjustment of her doona to make sure she's covered, a sense of jealously that her contorted sleeping position and still functioning shoulders won't require a fifteen minute wake up routine complete with groaning that sounds like a couple of amorous possums going at it!

It's then quite a few minutes later and I find myself still sitting in her room, on the end of her bed staring at her with tears running down my face, completely dumbstruck that something so perfect could ever have been entrusted to me by the universe. (Karma really dropped the ball with this one!) A bloke who listed his major accomplishments as lifting moderately heavy things and being able to consume roughly 1.73 times his own body weight in all the major food groups.

I've found all kinds of wonderful surprises in Charlie's developing personality and especially in my own. There's a Leo Tolstoy quote I love, "There is no past and no future; no one has ever entered those two imaginary kingdoms. There is only the present." This is the mantra for connection, for true listening, the right here right now you matter most that our kids need to know without doubt.

5. ***Sundays:*** Out of these five opportunities, sometimes when the stars align, work commitments are easy, and the house does not resemble a black op training ground hitting all five seems like the easiest thing in the world. Other times, one out of five is all that I can manage, except the non–negotiables, and this and always will remain: SUNDAYS.

Sundays started off as Charlie's day while navigating the divorce as I did not want to waste a single minute of my limited time with this kid. Charlie gets to pick and choose everything about the day: what we do, what we wear, where we go and even what we eat. I'm constantly amazed by Charlie's choices and her self-restraint that I definitely would not have shown given this amount of freedom at her age. In fact, I STILL can't be trusted at an all-you-can-eat-buffet. It is also a great opportunity for Charlie to learn to make great choices as I believe she won't learn to make good choices by following orders.

Charlie might not hear everything I tell her but she see's everything I do. She looks to me for how to respond to life and its challenges, what to value and what to dismiss. She looks at me for examples of love, honesty and empathy and she looks to me for what is important. She must know without doubt, without question, and without hesitation, that her time with me is HER time.

I often ask, *who is getting the best of you? Is it work? Is it colleagues? Or is it your phone?*

I'm not saying I have all of the answers or this will work for you, however, I believe that what we as parents need is to reset, refocus and hold ourselves accountable. We all have fears, hopes and dreams, some based in reality, some from experience and others possibly from eating a spicy pizza before bed.

Charlie and I love Valentine's day, if for any other reason that we have a legitimate reason to have waffles and ice cream covered in chocolate.

I get asked so often if I think we really need a special day to profess our love with some grand gesture complete with jewellery, flowers, chocolates or even some specialty, purpose designed, hardly practical but unusually interesting underwear?

Valentine's day has its origins in the Roman festival of Lupercalia. The festival celebrated the coming of spring. It also included fertility rites and the pairing off of women and men by a lottery, sort of an ancient *Tinder* by the sounds of it.

A quick survey sees people firmly divided into two camps.

Let me explain why I'm in both.

We have Mother's Day and Father's Day; specific and important dates to make a fuss and show our gratitude and love for our parents. *Do we need these dates? Shouldn't every day be a celebration of our parents?*

In fact, those of you reading this with a birthdate around the 14th of November may well be the by-product of your parent's handywork after a romantic Valentine's dinner and chocolates while wearing the purpose designed, hardly practical but unusually interesting underwear.

Just stop and consider that. Or don't.

Now I've managed to get that last thought out of my mind, let's try and focus on the bigger picture. Don't let the over-the-top commercialism detract from the importance and symbolism of setting aside one day a year to emphasis romance with your partner and role model positive expressions of love to your kids.

Every day is Valentine's Day when you have a daughter. It is up to us dads to support and prepare our daughters transition from princess towards one day having their own relationships and their own kids should they decide. Be the example with your standards.

Every day is Valentine's Day because It's up to us dads to model and help our daughters develop the skills and attitudes that will lead to more satisfying relationships. By making sure they know they're loved and lovable. To give them the confidence to choose partners who are good to them and good for them. Set the standard with your example.

Every day is Valentine's Day because we have got to accept that our daughters are going to want to date. It is important for our daughters, once they enter their teenage years to learn how to date, navigate romantic and sexual encounters, and to build healthy boundaries and relationships with those partners. Our daughters shouldn't have to work for love, not with us, and definitely not with any future partner. Our daughters need to see the example of love not being conditional on certain behaviours, compliance, or convenience. Be the example.

Every day is Valentine's Day because we must realise that our daughters are always watching and that what we do matters way more than what we say. We need to be asking ourselves what are our daughters learning about life in general, about morality, about how people should treat one another, about relationships from observing us every day. Set the standard.

Every day is Valentine's Day for me because getting a surprise bunch of flowers makes Charlie's day. Because I realise, I'm setting the standard she will accept from future partners. I must be the example. Because I realise I'm her example of how someone who loves and respects her should treat her. Because I realise I need to support and nurture who she really is and not try to control or create who I think she should be because the thought of anyone controlling this kid breaks my heart. I must do better. Be the example.

Every day is Valentine's Day when you realise the way you speak to your daughter will become her inner voice, her self-esteem, her confidence. It is all down to you. The way she perceives herself and others will reflect the values you display, the way you react and even the lunchbox notes you write. You do better. Set the standard.

Simply stated, it's up to us dads to make every day Valentine's Day and show our daughters how they should be treated. It is up to us dads to model respectful treatment of all women including not denigrating or disrespecting their mothers, because that example will set the standard.

So, on this Valentine's Day there will definitely be flowers, chocolates and a huge fuss made for my daughter. And every other moment, of every other day, I will be trying my hardest to be the example and set the standard.

Our family is mad for Christmas and the planning starts as early as the decorations in the supermarkets. There is the tree that needs to be dusted off and the lights unravelled and unknotted. Have you noticed how you think you are the most patient person and then you get the job of unravelling fairy lights? I've learned that you can cuss really loud as long as you use your inside voice while smiling on the outside and listening to 'All I want for Christmas' by Mariah Carey.

The covert plans for Jingles (Elf on the Shelf) to return consumes my waking hours and I already start planning the elaborate mischief that she will be getting up to. I will regale you with a few tales after I get to why Christmas is so important. We are not religious, but it is the awe and the utter belief that Charlie has in Santa, Jingles, the family get together that we have every Christmas day. Her excitement to be spending the day in the pool with her cousins and the food, the promise of Nans legendary home-made pavlova and loads of other desserts.

I work early mornings and over the Christmas holidays I relish the early morning calls from Charlie explaining in detail the antics of Jingles. I thought that taking Charlie out when she was younger was a black ops event. Well, let me tell you, planning and executing of some of the scenes takes the razor precision of a sniper, the stealth of a tight rope walker and the imagination of a ballet unicorn wearing stilettos.

In the hustle and bustle of bedtime routine, there is usually wild talk and rumination about what Jingle 'may' do and which unsuspecting dolls or toys will be roped into the mischief. It is usually a tiny little bear wearing a little jumper who is the willing accomplice and instigator of the shenanigans.

There have been many a night when I suddenly sit bolt upright, swearing and cursing about that so-and-so elf! Dragging myself out of my comfortable bed and sneaking through the house I find myself paging through my saved Pinterest ideas to maintain the previous elaborate scenes. Every year in the lead up to Jingles return, I secretly hope that Charlie will let on that she knows it has been me that has orchestrated all of the mischief and mayhem and we can finally relegate Jingles to the spools of fond childhood memories from which she can draw on to build her own traditions.

However, I immediately become caught up in the magic and wonder that is Charlie's reality. I secretly hope that we can get another year out of this tradition. It is like reading a fantastic novel that you are completely and utterly absorbed in, a novel that suspends the daily grid, the normal worries that completely captivates your imagination and changes your perception of reality, the constant reminder that as you progress through the pages of magic you know that you are coming to the end. You never want it to end, you never want to find out how it ends but there is that urge to predict the ending coupled with the need to know how it ends. The bittersweet realisation that the control is no longer ours, we just have to let it run its course. We need to realise we don't write our children's story; our children need to be the authors of their own story and with a bit of luck my role in Charlie's story could be as a side-kick and maybe even a mentor — hopefully not a villain.

What I have realised with Charlie, as perfect as each age has seemed and the desire for time to stand still, each new age, new experience, new change in her makes me excited and curious to see what is next. You never know when the first time will happen or the last time will happen with kids, they change so quickly.

One of my favourite traditions is not a particular Hallmark holiday but rather a simple day of the week. For as long as Charlie has graced Earth with her presence, Friday nights have been owned solely by us. After supper we will make a bowl of popcorn and jump into my bed and watch an episode of Vet on the Hill, complete with Charlie's diagnosis of the outcomes of surgeries, treatments, and medications. The fact that this kid knows that a linear foreign body causes peritonitis in a cat astounds me. I will mention that I won't dare question her accuracy and risk having her jumping out of bed to return with one of her many reference books that are well-thumbed and indexed to walk me through my obvious ignorance when it comes to animal anatomy.

It's the idle chatter, it's the closeness, its forgetting that the world around us exists and it is just being together.

One of the fondest memories I have of an early childhood tradition is the lunchbox notes that I started hiding in Charlie's lunchbox when we transitioned from being together every moment of the day to her traversing into kindergarten.

So, instead of me crying over the lost daddy-daughter time I decide to include these love notes in her lunch box. But don't be fooled - cry I did, and still do!

The main reason I did it was the reaction that it would elicit when she opened her lunch box to a surprise note that might just for a moment reconnect us even though we were apart. Looking back, I realise that it was more of a benefit for me as I distinctly remember eating my lunch and wondering if she was laughing at my silly notes that I had snuck into her lunch box without her seeing it.

Some of the notes were my world-renowned and show-stopping funny dad jokes. Others were declarations of love and pride. Some were continuations of the previous night bedtime stories and the hidden lesson. I have done more arts and crafts creating her lunch box notes than I did in junior academia.

The highlight of this tradition was when I started finding the very same notes in MY lunch that she had hidden before bed the night before. It is in moments like these when you see yourself in the actions of your mini me, slightly cuter, but only marginally shorter, that you realise they are watching everything you do, and it is in this realisation that, if I am going to raise a good person, I am actually going to have to be a better person – example is everything. It does make me wonder though, who's example was she following when she innocently asked the waiter to 'pull her finger' when we went for cake the other day? I'm not exaggerating when I say I was mortified!

My absolute favourite thing about what I do is the privilege of listening to people tell me in great detail about their relationships with their fathers and the indelible memories of their traditions and the impact that these seemingly fleeting moments had on them. However, they are anything but temporary. These moments in time can last generations as they are told to children and their children's children.

I get so caught up in the true and raw emotion of these memories, to be able to share and connect in the vivid recount of songs, tastes and feelings. It is so simple in its simplicity, the similar experiences of

Christmas mornings, the Easter egg hunts where dad bellowed with laughter while we all ran to harvest the eggs in the back yard.

Spending the day with dad at work and passing him all manner of tools and thingy-ma-jigs that I had no idea what they did, yet, I felt like an integral part of whatever it was that I didn't understand but no less vital to the successful outcome.

Dads that were both the sharers and keepers of secrets; just between us. Dads that were the sounding board for the inevitable confusions that needed a safe confidant to try and gain some clarity. Dads signature dishes in the kitchen and signature dance moves to music that we thought was archaic and so not cool that now transport us back to our lounge room. Dads that would make us recoil with the 'Eeew' when he and mum did the kissy face.

It's all about creating fond, firm, and lasting memories because that's where we will live forever in the hearts, minds and lives of our children.

I always ask Dads, *what sort of dad do you want to be and how do you want to be remembered? What stories will your children tell about you?*

Those memories will be a rock-solid anchor in trying times, a template, a standard and the medium in which we've planted the seeds of the garden from where their lives will grow.

How will you be remembered by your children?

WHO KNEW?

Chapter Six

Parenting does not change you.

It reveals who you really are.

"I've come to the conclusion this parenting gig doesn't get easier because your child matures.

It's hopefully because we do as parents."

Michael Ray

There is a constant theme that seems to appear in the discussions that I have with both mums, dads and even mates – and I am sure that most dads of daughters hear them too – the old chestnuts about rules for dating my daughter, puberty, and a myriad of other queries relating to the tween years and the transition into the mine-field that is teenage-hood and how I will cope with these apparently traumatic, emotional and challenging times. People telling me that I should relish the simple times because, "Oh boy, was I in for a surprise."

Each warning almost seemed to teeter on the edge of genuine concern and a gleeful hope of disaster that this next milestone could finally be the spanner in the works that sees my run of luck of having the easiest kid alive finally come to an end. And I can understand the undercurrent of doubt; surely these are important life skills that are normally handled by someone with actual experience of being a young girl who has navigated through this stage in their life and not some Peter Pan dad.

If I distil down the hours of advice, I can basically summarise the outcomes into two basic answers:

Mums' advice - "Michael, we are always here to lend a hand, so please don't hesitate to call and we will help anyway possible." (gotta love my mum tribe!)

Bro advice - Can best be described using a spectrum beginning from –

"I dunno. Good luck with that," to some age-old classic approaches including:

- Locking her up until she's thirty-years-old?
- Sending her to a convent?

- Anything you do to my daughter I'll do to you?
- Taking him into the backyard and showing a shallow grave you've prepared?
- Answering the door when he knocks with a shotgun in hand?
- Letting him know you can make him go away?

Let me start by saying that I in no way consider myself qualified to be the adult in charge of guiding this amazing little girl through life but as it's just Charlie and me. It's 100 percent up to me as her dad.

I am, however, probably overqualified after a lifetime of working as a bouncer, weight lifter, and boxer, to take on the role of the classic and outdated 'Overprotective, Scary Dad', as clearly proposed by the 'bro-advice', the only problem with this is if no one can ever date my daughter without fearing the barrel of a shotgun pointed at them, she is going to rebel anyway, She will learn I can't be trusted and won't talk to me and miss the opportunity to develop those skills in her teens while she's still young and has me nearby to help give advice.

As I have said before, I certainly am no 'woke bloke' and this has encouraged me to do a fair amount of reading for mere self-improvement and to try and understand the workings of my little grey matter and to try an understand what gets the synapses firing. I stumbled across an incredible study that discusses the effects of a father on a daughter's growth and development. A fascinating set of data repeatedly linked absentee dads to poor relationship outcomes for daughters (something mothers need to consider if they choose not to foster & support a father's relationship if separated), including high rates of unplanned pregnancy and divorce.

These studies show that there is a direct relationship between a dad's behaviour and his daughter's sexual and social development.

> The obstacles are always opportunities for growth.

This research suggests, daughters that grow up with fathers who disappointed them are more likely to interpret the intentions of other men as sexual when they grow up.

Being who I am this little nugget of information fuelled the fire to delve deeper into this subject to understand the importance of a father being involved and present in a daughter's life. The discussion paper covered how fathers influence their daughters' odds of risky sexual behaviour that are inexplicably associated with the particulars of so called 'daddy issues'. The most eye-opening fact was that even daughters that had a 'present' father while growing up, the memories of how their fathers disappointed them actually primed them for promiscuity.

So, as I interpret the study, basically it is not only the involvement that I have with Charlie that will benefit her and her development but rather the actual investment and true presence. Therefore, the stereotypical 'Scary Dad' is not an option that has any chance of achieving good outcomes for me and handing it completely off to the mothers (if that's an option) doesn't really gel with unconditional, do anything for my kid's type parenting we all like to think we are capable of. Does it?

It's up to us dads to be the example of how our daughters should be treated.

It is up to us dads to model respectful treatment of women including not denigrating or disrespecting their mothers if you are separated.

It is up to us dads to support and prepare our daughters transition from our little girls towards one day having their own relationships and their own kids should they decide.

It's even up to us dads not to presume our child's sexual orientation as this may cause harm down the road when the child starts to reconcile their sexuality with what their parents expect from them. This can be very painful and make the coming out process harder than it may already be.

Simply put, it's up to us dads!

Charlie will be marrying a myriad of people within a week, everyone from her best friend to the dog! I love seeing her work through the abstract idea of love and marriage and watch how she perceives the adult constructs.

> If you're uncomfortable talking with your kids about anything it's more to do with your relationship and the connection than the topic.

I've got to accept that Charlie is going to want to date. It is important for Charlie, once she enters her teenage years to learn how to date, navigate romantic and sexual encounters, and to build healthy boundaries and relationships with those partners.

Charlie is my daughter and like every father, I think she is beautiful. Not anymore, nor any less, than any other girls. Like every father I'm gripped by fear, the desire to protect her — body and soul.

I look at Charlie now at nine-years-old and it's easier to see the girl she's becoming than the baby she once was. Apart from her smile and her sparkling eyes, that baby is gone forever replaced by this funny little person in her own right.

I look at her and see the little girl she is and I currently believe she still needs to be protected and nurtured, but the harsh reality is I won't be around to protect her forever. However, the lessons learned will hopefully take her into her adult life.

As much as I'd like to keep my precious bub wrapped safely in my arms, I know it's like trying to hold back the tide and one day she'll be a young woman. I hope with a strength of body and mind, a beautiful kind soul, and with dreams for the future. I hope that wonderful energy will attract people into her life that are just like her and can add new dimensions and perspectives.

I want her to be adored − body, mind and soul by someone other than family. After all we are all just biased parents, aren't we?

Yes, I absolutely want her to find a partner in life that sees her magic as I do. Yes, when the time is right, I would love grandkids, however, being fifty years older than Charlie, time may not be on my side.

I want to show her that how she looks does not matter and is not something she should seek validation for. I want her to know someone will love her not because her body is beautiful, but because her soul is beautiful. Charlie should learn that her value is equal to that of any man she knows regardless of whether he finds her attractive.

It's up to me as Charlie's parent, to make sure she is confident and in control, to make responsible informed decisions about her own body, to love herself just as she is. Whether it is teaching Charlie the accurate names for her body parts (I beam with pride when Charlie can point out her tibia, fibula, and femur). We don't call her head 'up there' so why would we call her vagina 'down there'?

They're not 'adult' words to be off limits until some arbitrary age or until poor old dad here can cope. Educating Charlie about menstruation or discussing sexual behaviour as she is getting ready for a date is all in my future and dodging, squirming, and wincing aren't reactions that are going to help her feel comfortable in her own skin or confident about who she is.

It really does help having seventeen odd animals that are oblivious to 'behind closed doors' activities. Being gardening enthusiasts and spending many hours outside, Charlie regularly shouts out proudly how she has two bugs that are 'mating'. I am sure at this juncture that she is not sure as to what that means, but is perfectly comfortable telling me, usually in an octave louder than is generally acceptable in a built-up area and bringing me the copulating bugs to investigate with her.

I firmly believe that we will never have to sit down and have 'the talk'. I believe that the subject will be broached as she matures and the relevant information that is age and emotionally appropriate will be openly discussed. I secretly think that this is what all the mums and dads were referring to when they want to know how I was going to cope with Charlie's transition into teenage-hood.

> Your situation and circumstance are where innovation and adaptation thrive because of constraints.

As Dads, I feel we should not wince over things we are proud of or happy about in our kids and this Charlie already understands. When I'm proud of her and happy for her I grin like an idiot. I tear up – as is now an expectation, much to her distaste and dramatic eye-roll.

Although, I still have yet to figure out how she doesn't like the raucous whistling and shouting of appreciation and pride when she receives student of the week. I stand at the back of the hall quietly and only when her name is called do I perform the wild cry of the 'proud dad'— this is something that I hope she adopts and carries on as a tradition.

Back to topic and 'the talk'. So, if I reveal my discomfort with Charlie's sexuality, I'm unintentionally teaching her it's either something to be afraid of or something to be disdained.

I'll also be directly or indirectly teaching her that I don't want to be involved in knowing that part of her and that will probably create distance in our relationship. None of this will improve her self-esteem or her ability to believe I love her unconditionally.

Charlie deserves to have my confidence in her and in the lessons she's learnt from the example I've set. Charlie deserves better. She deserves to live life on her own terms and follow her dreams. Charlie simply cannot do that from a helpless victim mindset. She must one day make her own decisions and own the consequences so it is critical that I teach my daughter to solve problems now and not hope she will just figure it out down the road.

I could easily sit back and listen to every problem Charlie has and offer what I think is an acceptable solution. However, what does Charlie learn from that other than I am obviously the smartest dad in the whole world? Which is already a well-established fact requiring no further validation!

As Charlie's dad, I have no choice once she is older but to support her decisions. That support doesn't mean, 'solve her problem'. It means to support her decisions and wait to be asked if she needs me to intervene. This is a lesson I'm only starting to learn now and is by far the hardest yet, I realise now as much as it pains me, I must raise Charlie to leave me and be who she is.

Thinking I can control Charlie's choices when she's older is like the bloke riding the elephant at the circus; it might look like he's in control but the minute that elephant wants to do something that bloke is nothing but a passenger! Therefore, there will definitely be rules for dating my daughter; those rules simply stated, will be hers and hers alone.

I have found that by paying attention to myself as much as to Charlie, the realisation only one of us is developmentally equipped to respond rather than react, and this I believe has inadvertently enrolled me the greatest self-improvement course ever designed.

Parenting does not get easier because your child matures and learns to be a person, it's you who has hopefully matured and grown to be a parent.

I need to be honest enough to put aside my ego and ask what part I am playing as a parent in my child's behaviour rather than blaming external influences such as social media, peer pressure and the like. The fact that

I can constantly identify possible external influences on Charlie's behaviours also indicates there is an opportunity to prepare her for them and how I perceive them will affect her. Understanding and then communicating my core values is the fundamental aspect of me becoming an effective parent. I believe that parents who are aware of their values, convey them clearly, and act in alignment with them set the example for our children.

For values or guiding principles to be truly effective they have to be verbs. It's not 'integrity,' it's 'always do the right thing.' It's not 'empathy,' it's 'imagine how you would feel if someone treated you like that'. Articulating our values as verbs indicates we have a clear idea of how to act in any situation.

> The exposure to appropriate and meaningful struggle and stress is the catalyst from which strength, resilience and fulfillment are borne.
>
> Hard isn't a fact. It's an attitude.

I have been embroiled in a VCAT issue with some previous unscrupulous business partners that has required a few years of back and forth and Charlie has been privy to the process. About a year into the process, while I was sitting getting the reams of paperwork completed for submission, she asked me why I no longer had my gym and why I was no longer friends with the other shareholders. I was once again struck about how innocently and simply a child will interpret a situation. My stresses and strains were parallel to her best friend taking her Beanie Boo and no longer wishing to play with her. It was with this analogy that I explained the situation. She needed to know that this was not a disagreement because I wanted something. This was a disagreement because of what was right and just. I wanted Charlie to know that there was a time and place to pick the battles that would win the war. Winning the war was not the aim; it is standing up and fighting for what you believe.

As parents we are leaders and as leaders we can either manipulate our children's behaviours or we can inspire them by our examples, values, and actions.

> "If your actions inspire others to dream more, learn more, do more and become more, you are a leader."
> John Quincy Adams

As parents and as leaders, you should ground yourself in values that last like honesty, hard work, responsibility, fairness, generosity, and respect for others. You won't get it right every time – you'll make mistakes like we all do. But if you listen to the truth that's inside yourself, even when it's hard, even when it's inconvenient, people will notice. They'll gravitate towards you. And you'll be part of the solution instead of part of the problem.

Trust is maintained when values and beliefs are actively managed. If parents do not actively work to keep clarity, discipline and consistency in balance, then trust starts to break down. Leading or parenting means our children will willingly follow us — not because they must, but because they want to. Connection and respect are everything.

I was sitting at my desk pondering this very book on a day that Charlie had two little friends over. The tent was out, the fairy lights twinkling, the fish and chips had been consumed and the three of them were playing in the back yard collecting bugs, digging holes and playing what kids play.

In our house we have a decadent jar of lollies that is always around for a mid-night snack or an after-dinner treat. I was sitting mesmerised by the sound of the laughter and the endless chatter of the girls playing and was bought back to reality with Charlie's shout-whisper to her friends, "Please go and put that back. If you want a lolly just ask my Dad."

I said and did nothing and just continued to listen to the exchange. The lolly jar was returned as quietly as a dinosaur tip-toeing on bubble wrap and nothing else was said. The nights shenanigans continued.

The next day after we had delivered the friends to their home amongst loads of "Aah's" and "Can't we stay another night?" Returning home to try and return the house to some order of semblance, we chattered about how great the night was and how we needed to immediately get onto organising the next soiree and deciding on the menu and the days schedule, there was a lull in the conversation. Charlie piped in, "Dad, can I tell you something?" Her new recent catch phrase to my standard answer, "Of course Bubs."

"So, last night while we were outside the girls took the lolly jar out of the cupboard," she said. I remained silent and let her continue. "I asked them to put it back and to ask you if they wanted one as you always say yes," she said.

"WHAT?" I shouted. "I do not always say YES!"

Charlie was quiet for a bit; I could see the little cogs in her brain interpreting my response. She then roared with laughter and that was all that was needed to be said.

WHO KNEW?

Chapter Seven

Contemporary Fathering.

"*Leave work loud and leave proud*, showing colleagues that it is okay, in fact absolutely the right thing, for a father to collect his child from school,
attend sports day, etc."

Michael Ray

Before Charlie came into the world and for the first few years, I worked in a hypermasculine environment as a high-performance strength and conditioning coach and also doing a lot of personal security for rock stars that came through the Australian nightclubs and bands along with all the stereotypical bloke stuff. This was not really the ideal and textbook preparation for being a father. If I'm honest, I think my entire preparation for being a father was my mum saying to me maybe once or twice, "wait until you have kids." Sagely advise that I believe most men growing up in my era received from their parents. It was sort of the same as parents smacking you on the side of the head when you did nothing wrong while proclaiming, "that is what you would get if you DID do something."

With Charlie's arrival there is a great deal that I learned. I learnt that when I was younger in this hypermasculine environment, the majority of what I was doing was basically trying to fit in, trying to belong.

I've realised that I was trying to belong to a bunch of blokes that were trying to belong to a bunch of blokes who were also trying to belong to a bunch of blokes, and no one actually knew who they were or what they wanted.

We were following a script that we thought was the masculine norm. And since having been in the space that I'm in now speaking with fathers and a lot of men, some of them suffering quite significant challenges in life, it all turned out to be a facade.

I'm really glad that I've been able to cast this off. Fatherhood has actually allowed me to discover who I am as a man and especially as a parent. And a lot of the stuff from my youth, when I look back, was just wasted. Not a regret sort of wasted, but rather wasted out of pure ignorance of anything better or more constructive.

As Marcel Proust said, "the challenge isn't seeing new destinations but seeing the same things with new eyes," and that's really what happened when I look back and see how desperately I had internalised any real values.

It was all a matter of trying to fit in, trying to be one of the crowd; one of the boys. I was following a crowd that was following the crowd that was taking us nowhere. With the arrival of Charlie, the haze and directionless ambling of the crowd disappeared, and the clarity of purpose and direction appeared.

I get asked how I landed with the moniker 'Solo Dad'. It was because there was a huge and sudden rush to conflate me with men's rights activists in which I am the furthest from. I find many of them so frightening and toxic and just horrific with some of their beliefs that they espouse.

At the onset of my career as an activist I do believe that there was a modicum of mistrust and it was implied that I was either trying to get more access to my child or that I was somehow embittered by my situation, rather than me actually fighting for the rights of my daughter and trying as best as a besotted and doting dad to prepare the way for her as best as possible.

I also made a conscious choice to stay single after Charlies Mum left. I couldn't take the risk of someone getting attached to Charlie and vice versa, only for it to end down the track. I realised that the huge age gap between Charlie and I would result in Charlie being without me for more years that she had me, and for this reason I wanted to soak up and enjoy every minute with her. Fortunately, I had so many wonderful, amazing, supportive female friends, so Charlie didn't run short of female play dates and support, shopping, nails and hair excursions.

On a selfish personal level, I just didn't want to let someone else get attached. I think a lot of the times many women who were interested, were more interested in being Charlie's replacement mum than they were being my partner. And it wasn't fair on them either. That's the main reason for the 'Solo Dad'. To make it clear, I wasn't in that men's rights activists club. I wanted to show people that if I can do it, anyone can.

When I became a parent, I was learning all about that good stuff because I was doing my coaching training at the time. So, I hadn't worked out what my values were up until that point. I was on a twin track of learning how to become the best version of myself through the lens of becoming a coach and also becoming the best version of myself through becoming a parent. And, I found the two tracks wonderfully enriching but difficult at times, because we don't always want to find out everything about ourselves. Lots of people go through life in happy denial. I think of who they are and that's what sits under the surface.

I'm learning all the time. Learning more about myself and learning about the impact that I have on others. If having a child doesn't change you in an instant, you're really missing the journey that childhood is because you see yourself reflected back.

There are so many occasions where I see myself in Charlie; her mannerisms, her sayings, her sass! I listen to Charlie playing with her friends and listen to the young babble and to hear my words clearly being regurgitated. This shows that these little people are like sponges and we have to be aware of what we say and how we act because they will become the embodiment of us. It's because she's trying to mimic what I do that her sense of self comes from the examples that I set.

I've learnt from some brilliant coaches; my dad was the best that I could ever hope for my hero, he truly inspired me. I remember that he would always say, "If that's what you want to do, I'll back you, but you weigh the consequences. If it goes wrong and you know. Think about it."

And that's what I say to Charlie, "I'm learning to be a dad, just like you're learning to be a kid. We've got to work these things out together." I know it sounds biased, but I'm blessed with the easiest kid in the world, so I don't want to make it that I am some parenting guru. I've just got a really, really easy kid. And I think because it was just her and I for those five years, she knows her contributions matter.

And it's no different to building a team or a business. When I work with elite level teams, it is all about building the team and the team values and how you fit into the team.

Charlie and I are a team. Like a team we need to have clear communication where nothing is out of bounds. We have respect and we have boundaries, and there is never any subject that is taboo. I tell Charlie, "If I say something that you don't think is right, I need you to tell me."

The last thing I want is for Charlie to buckle to peer pressure or stereotypes or social norms. Charlie will be placed in situations and circumstances where she will have to make a stand, or she may feel the daunting pressure of that peer pressure. I can only hope that because of the foundation that we have created while growing and learning together that I become that little voice in the back of her head when someone's asking her to do something she feels is not right or she feels that she may compromise herself or do something that just doesn't seem right. It's very much one eye on the task at hand but the vision firmly on the future and how it's going to shape her life.

When the doctor doled out the prognosis after the accident, suddenly my house that I built and furnished throughout my life had become a burning house with flames leaping through the roof, smoke billowing out the windows, and in that instant, I was forced to decide what was I prepared to rush in and save? And the only thing that came to mind was what effect this was going to have on my daughter. Nothing else mattered.

All of the work, all of the possessions, all of the position and the prestige that went with travelling with the team just didn't mean anything because I would actually sacrifice time with her.

The great thing now is that I rearranged everything and now I'm able to work for the same amount of money and not lose any time with Charlie. Once I set my values, and this was to prioritise and protect my time with her, my situation and circumstances allowed me to be innovative and move everything into three days a week.

I'm in a unique position where I get to sit in groups of mums and dads as somebody with a completely different perspective and subjective reality. I remember something from a movie that Charles Baudelaire said, *"The best deception the devil ever perpetrated was convincing people he didn't exist."*

I believe a lot of women that I communicate with inadvertently support the patriarchy in a roundabout way with things like 'maternal instinct', 'only a mother's love', 'mother knows best', where they are pigeonholing themselves into all of those extra pressures.

When a woman is struggling with the normal frustrations of raising an infant, whether it be breastfeeding, colic, or sleep deprivation for example, these are essentially natural struggles that come with parenting. Everything becomes overbearing, but it seems that women suffer under this pressure a bit more because of the stereotypical expectations of maternal instinct.

For me it was so different. I was basically an idiot. In fact, I still am. Nobody expected anything unbelievable from me. As long as I put the nappy on in some sort of a traditional fashion and it stayed on, and I managed to keep Charlie alive and didn't drop her too often then I was the most amazing, wonderful dad. However, it is rarely the case with mums. I believe that by buying into all of this man-guilt, mum-shame, and all the rest of this archaic thinking, mums feel like they should be better at everything and simply cope without discussion as it is supposed to be the predetermined primal instinct. Or is it simple social expectation?

Being a Solo Dad and having to cope I can honestly say I think there's definitely a parental instinct, the need to nurture and protect; that feeling that your heart just wants to melt. I remember clearly the day Charlie was handed over to me and I held this tiny, pink, wriggling little human with the smallest nose and tiniest toes. The wash started at the top of my head and slowly spilled over my whole body — the only apt description that I can think of is when you down a gulp of neat whiskey and you feel that heat radiate through every fibre of your body.

It's documented that when babies are born or during pregnancy, fathers' hormones actually change. There is an increase in oxytocin, our testosterone drops, and we suddenly become the best joke tellers. Who knew?

When women suffer under this misnomer, 'maternal instinct', they're judged so much more harshly than the 'bumbling dad'. The first thing that is implied is that they will be responsible for the upbringing of the child and will take on the household responsibilities and Dads will default to the provider and breadwinner.

This outdated reference chips away at both Mum's and Dad's choices and confidence — the preconceived gender roles that society expects. I think that this is driven greatly by the individual's upbringing and the amount of family dynamic. I know that I defaulted to the quintessential protector and breadwinner role when Charlie was born, and I was THE BEST assistant that ever thronged this planet. I fetched. I carried. I provided. I protected. I was man — Hear Me Roar!

But all it seems to do is cause resentment in Mums and it makes men second guess themselves and default into assistant or pain in the butt or at best another child to pander to for the first few months.

When chatting with a dad, he was saying that he tries so hard to be as accommodating as possible when it comes to the home. He shared the story of how third world war almost erupted in the house when his partner asked him when he got home from work what he would like for dinner. To ensure that he did not add too much extra stress or pressure, he simply replied, "I'm easy hun, anything." He tells how he could see his partners usual rosy complexion take on a bright red hue, her left eye started twitching and the jaw started to clench and relax. He looked on helplessly not knowing quiet what he had said wrong. He winced and waited for the outburst. Through clenched teeth his partner hissed at him. "All I am asking you is for your input. I am asking you to simply participate in the household drudgery. Sometimes I just want the decision to be taken from me. I just want you to be involved. I would like you to make a suggestion when I ask you next time. If I feel that it is too involved, or I don't have the ingredients, I will just tell you."

Who knew that he was being perceived as being dismissive when he thought he was being helpful? Dads need to take responsibility and not simply defer.

The involvement spills over into caring for the children; you are not simply there to be the disciplinarian and provider. You are seesaw, castle, horse, storyteller, bather, clean room assistant and the list is not exhaustive. There is nothing wrong with having two different parenting styles because through life children are going to have friends with different styles, bosses with different styles, co-workers with different styles, and there's nothing wrong with adding a different dynamic to the parenting of the children. Its counterproductive to undermine each other. There's nothing wrong with having the same outcome through different approaches. These outdated gender expectations cause massive harm and are holding us all back as a society. When we speak about 'only a mother's love'. I've had women say, "Oh, but I carried the child for nine months. I created this child."

Are we saying the biology is the prerequisite for love? I can never speak or profess to understand what a woman goes through while carrying these little miracles and I can never speak of childbirth, but I can speak of the undeniable and unfaltering love and bond that I have for Charlie. I usually ask women if they would ring their dads and say that, "I understand that you couldn't possibly love me as much as Mum because you didn't carry me. But that's okay. Because you're a man." *Will you look at your son or brother and think, great guy but simply not going to love and care for his children as well as his partner because he's a man and did not carry the child?*

I certainly cannot and will not speak of or doubt any women's bond and undeniable love for their children, however, it does amaze me how we speak with great clarity and confidence about other people's reality.

I love a compliment as much as the next guy, probably a little bit more, but some of the praise and compliments I get are bordering on patronising. I remind those that are quick to comment that, "I'm just being a parent." And when people say, "you're a great dad," I'd rather say, "No, I want to be a good parent because the bar for dads is a lot lower than what it is for mums. I'd like to be seen as a present, competent and engaged parent."

> If your behaviour is governed or influenced by what is typical, expected or popular, rather than by what is required for your family, ethical and authentic, you don't have a problem with your masculinity, you have a problem with your character.

It's a gender thing. Society does not see fathers as caregivers and unfortunately neither do many fathers.

According to The Australian Institute of Family Studies a mere 5% of fathers take primary parental leave. This is often cited as an indication that fathers aren't interested, aren't able or both, to be held equally responsible for raising the next generation.

Let me digress for a minute and examine 'primary and secondary caregivers'. This arbitrary labelling of parents is one of my pet-peeves. I am obviously not clever enough to understand the advantage of having this classification for caregivers.

Surely a secondary caregiver is a grandparent, a babysitter or child carer. As parents we are both primary caregivers.

As a solo dad, I am classified as the primary caregiver regardless, yet somehow my breadwinning is considered separate from caregiving, so while I am earing the money to buy the bread, I am a secondary caregiver, once I am at home making the sandwich suddenly, magically, I am now a caregiver. Sounds confusing, doesn't it? Welcome to my world. Surely, breadwinning not only enables caregiving but for all mums who are shamed or feel guilt and have their choices questioned for wanting and having a great career, they are in fact providing examples for both their daughter to follow and their sons to embrace.

How much cultural harm through the primary and secondary classification is happening with the potential to diminish or denigrate the value of the relationship not only between father and child, but also between mother and employer?

The misguided use of the terms primary and secondary caregivers has allowed workplaces to willfully be blind to our parental responsibilities.

The majority of dads that I speak to overwhelmingly discuss how the workplace shapes the family dynamics and roles. If we look at the 5% of men taking parental leave as an indication that men are worried should they avail themselves of this entitlement, then it may harm their career, which will in turn, harm their family, as I am sure is the opposite side of the same coin for women. The 'motherhood penalty' which is an impact on career advancement and financial earnings is the opposite side of the coin of the 'fatherhood forfeit' – that sees fathers forfeit time, connection, involvement and the many irreplaceable milestones with their children.

Neither are acceptable or necessary by removing the outdated gender expectations and financial disincentives caused by these labels that has dads facing similar challenges to caregiving as mothers once had to entering the workforce.

It is one thing for an organisation to have policies that enable but we also need to have a culture that encourages and expects fathers to take advantage of these policies.

If you have team members bragging about working eighty hours a week and firing off emails at ten o'clock at night or being devalued with derogatory comments about enjoying a holiday when they decide to take paternity leave, surely then this is an illustration of what women have been saying for years about their unpaid, undervalued, caring responsibilities, and perhaps by fixing the culture within your organisation will do more to foster equality.

Puppies and kittens aren't just for Christmas and dads aren't just for parental leave.

WHO KNEW?

Chapter Eight

Breadwinner?

"There's so much joy in watching my daughter discover and search out her own interests with me simply being a willing accomplice. It's a second chance to view the world with excitement, enthusiasm and a boundless curiosity of how stuff happens."

Michael Ray

Frankly, men should find it patronising to be praised so highly for accomplishing everyday parenting tasks and calm down about dads doing normal stuff with their kids. If we keep making routine acts of fatherhood such a huge deal, boys will never learn that this bottle-making, baby-wearing, ballet bun-creating level of fatherhood isn't superhuman. It's what's expected of them.

Gender inequity is structural and systemic. It affects both women and men. It's not only about the jobs we hold, but it's also about cultural expectations and assumptions about family values. Today, the workplace and family are all in transition, yet most of our social norms were established in a bygone time. Ultimately, it is unrealistic to expect one part of our lives to change without completely disrupting the others. If Charlie is really going to break through all the glass ceilings, we will also need to let go of the incompetent dad stigma.

What challenges or opportunities are present for me raising Charlie in a family where there is no mother, no significant female role model? I keep hearing if Charlie is a 'daddy's girl' or if 'she has me wrapped around her little finger' I may hinder her growth as an independent and self-sufficient individual.

The time for change was years ago; the opportunity is right now. This crisis didn't create the problems for working parents and families, it merely exposed and exasperated them.

For too long too many have been happy to classify 'breadwinning' as somehow separate from caregiving rather than a vital and foundational part of it.

This single divisive and misguided approach has allowed workplaces to be willfully blind to not only our parental responsibilities, but also to our overriding WHY with regards to the importance of our careers.

I'm not sure where the bias is worse for a woman who's judged harshly for not focusing on a child or a man who acts harshly for not being able to care for a child because it's the opposite side of the same coin. Women are sometimes judged harshly for not putting one hundred percent into the kids while having a career. There is always that patronising under current that they are doing such a fabulous job at being a career woman and then the toxic implication of 'but what about the kids?'

It's these outdated gender expectations that are holding us all back and that have become glaringly obvious to me. The fact that we don't have change rooms in men's toilets and the fact that I think nearly every man at some stage has been challenged going into a parent's room to change their baby, as if we're not that welcomed or looked on with some sort of suspicion as to why we're in there.

For all the inequity that happens to women, there is a corresponding one that happens to men. In the talks I do, I give the example of a Venn Diagram – you know that little diagram with those circles that all meet in the middle and have the over-lapping areas that illustrate the logical relation between sets. In the diagram that I use there is circle with what women want, including a life outside the family and a circle with men, that desperately want to be involved in the family. The trick then is to decide how to determine the actions to take at this intersection that benefits everyone within the family unit.

We've been brought up in a society where we honestly believe, and I believe, that there's some secret sauce that mum knows, she should after all just slot into motherhood like it's natural, right? The terms, 'maternal instinct', 'only a mother's love', 'mother knows best', along with all of the marketing and the hallmark fetishized images of motherhood, casts Mums into an unrealistic role.

It's a learned skill; you learn to be a parent. It puts immense pressure on mums who may be struggling with all the normal frustrations of raising a child, whether it be colic or sleep deprivation or breastfeeding or even post-natal depression. They don't only impact a woman's perception of motherhood, but because women are groomed through life to become a mother, that it all becomes about mothering. Women then put themselves under immense pressure and see their inability to be this naturally maternal nurturer as failing somehow or being flawed as a woman, not only as a mum, whereas dads don't have that weight of expectation thrust upon them, we simply defer to mum all the time – "What should I do? How should I do this?" placing even more pressure on the woman as the presumption is that she knows what she is doing.

Like most young couples bringing home a baby, especially the first one, and having no previous experience, there's a fair chance that mum would have read a lot of books and completed research on motherhood, but that doesn't help if she feels that the baby is not responding in the way that the book says it should. Coupled with all of the well-meaning 'advice' that is offered from anyone who has had a child leaves the parents feeling hopelessly overwhelmed.

Like most first-time parents, the first time I was solely responsible for getting Charlie through the night, I admit I was terrified I would make a mistake. The first weeks of being a parent coupled with an unusually high anxiety level can really work you up about all the possible things that can go horribly wrong with a baby. I'd imagined more scenarios than the sum total of the 'Die Hard' movies. Suddenly, in my warped paranoid first-time dad brain I was John MacLaine with a chubby little cherub for a sidekick who wasn't going to be much use against any villains and unable to appreciate my snappy one-liners.

Man, woman or non-binary, your choice of partner is going to have a huge impact on your career and the structure of your home-life, and it will become the default for our children.

Up until this point, childcare was seen as a woman's issue. Affordable childcare is often cited as a barrier to women entering the workforce. It's a barrier for parents entering the workforce. So, we need to all get on board, from the top down, and all be together in the same team. That's what will make the difference and move this forward.

I know I used to go to school drop off dressed in my work uniform even though I had the day off because I didn't want people to think that I was an unemployed dad. And then it made me realize if I'm not, as they think I should be, if they see me as different, does it really matter? And then I finally thought, "you know, it only matters to my daughter. She's the only one that really counts." I was able to cast off the ego and all of a sudden what others thought didn't matter.

Your child can't tell the difference between your ego and your reality. So don't be that guy. Decide what sort of father you want to be, decide what stories you want your children to tell their children about you and just be that dad. It's that simple.

I believe that you've got to discuss being involved in the household with your partner if you want to be more hands on. You can't just impose your will. You've got to come to an agreement about what's right and what's wrong, where you can contribute. I often hear women talk about how useless their husbands are and how I wish he would do this right, or how they wish he would do that differently. I always like to ask if they have actually given him a chance? The standards that you hold him to.

Who's standards are these? Are these self-imposed standards and requirements that important? Is it that dreadful that you have a different approach that achieves the same outcome? As long as you're on the same page with the big picture, how you get there doesn't really matter.

Having different parenting styles is a great thing because for all your children's lives they're going to come across different policies, different teachers, different friends, that all have different personalities and different characteristics. So, as long as the big picture, the outcomes, the values, are all based on the same thing. And there's nothing wrong with one of you being the disciplinarian and one of you being the relaxed one as long as at the end of the day, it's who you authentically are.

I know that this is a chapter dedicated to Fathers, but I would love to share with you an experience that I recently had speaking in a Mums group. This was a group of solo parents like myself, mothers that had to fill the role of primary carer and primary breadwinner as described by the current outdated gender norms. It was not the story of why they had to fulfil both roles but rather the trial, tribulations and wins that they experienced.

These women held different positions based on their prior employment history and on the requirements of their families. Regardless of their positions the similarities between the emotional turmoil that these women felt and that of men in the same position was staggering.

The fact that they were more inclined to fabricate a reason for missing a day of work or having to leave early so as to hide the fact that they had a family engagement, the guilt that they felt because they missed most of the children after school activities and they were merely updated by friends or family that were enlisted to fetch, carry and watch. The guilt they felt when the kids 'played up' at night for no other reason than they wanted their mum's attention and they either had work to do, home responsibilities, or were too tired to even cook dinner.

Sadly, dads are seen or portrayed, especially in media, as a 'bumbling man–child', with no hope and is portrayed as another child for mum to have to look after, which just makes it worse.

Like Charlie noticed the packaging mostly depicting women, she has also noticed how modern sitcoms have a very derogatory depiction of fathers or men. She asked about The Simpsons while it was playing in the background as we were preparing dinner. She wanted to know why Homer was always at the pub and why he kept on throttling Bart and questioned, 'did all Dads fall asleep at work?'

There seems to be that the depiction that men are ill-suited for parenting which reinforces the need for the women to take on more responsibility. There is no harm in being able to have a good laugh at yourself, however, there is a fine line that divides humour and degradation.

We still have a real 'macho-man' type conception of men, but we also have nine suicides a day in Australia of which seven of them are men. We have over sixty-three thousand suicide attempts by men each year and we can see clearly preponderance of evidence.

It shows that the more gender equitable society is, the less mental health is a problem. When you look at Norway, they have one of the highest up takes of parental leave by men at 90% compared to our 5% and when measuring children's mental and physical health and academic and social skillsets they ranked in the top 3 in the world.

It gives me great hope knowing that those Norwegian blokes were not always so 'woke'. Before a four-week use-it-or-lose it paternal quota was introduced, less than 3% of men took paternity leave. How simple and how achievable is this? Who Knew?

The first point of contact for new parents here in Victoria is the 'MATERNAL and Child Health Centre'. I've never felt more like a third wheel than at these appointments. Why isn't this the 'PARENTAL and Child Health Centre'? With as many as 1 in 7 men suffering postnatal depression this is such a missed opportunity to screen men. A less than optimal dad is unable to assume his role as an equal parent and therefore adds more pressure to mum and could well damage the relationship and family dynamic going forward.

Even before the child is born there's massive challenges to dads being able to attend the numerous appointments because we aren't seen as 'necessary' by both employers and practitioners.

In a 2011 literature review on paternal involvement during pregnancy and labour, the authors claim that the preponderance of evidence suggests that dads who are actively involved and invested in the baby before he or she is born disproportionately remain involved in the child's life. I would love to see enshrined in workplace agreements and policies, the obligation for fathers to attend every scan, and appointment and possibly even be considered on the guest list for baby showers.

The systematic and structural changes needed to bring dads into the contemporary parenting role that is required are the result of so many factors that in total keep us locked in the outdated gender expectations and we all suffer – men, women and especially children.

We need to stop framing pregnancy and children as if they only affect women. Women don't just become mothers. We all become parents.

WHO KNEW?

Chapter Nine

Handbrake on the Drive for Equality

"We need to stop framing parenting as something that only affects women. For some reason parenting seems to be the last bastion that we haven't had a concerted effort to remove the gendered assumptions of a bygone time."

Michael Ray

I have written fondly about my dad and how he was the provider for the family and so it is only right that I know dedicate a few words to my incredible Mum. The woman that put up with my stubborn streak – I do want to mention that I believe I inherited this trait from her. The woman that answered so many late night calls that began with the phrase, "Don't worry, Michael is okay but…" The woman that banged down the door and insisted that I get back to the hospital after my 'little accident'. The woman that opened her home to me and Charlie. The woman that helps me fetch and carry Charlie when I have to work. The woman who does the shopping, cooks suppers and dotes on me, even at the ripe old age of fifty-eight.

Mum was born in 1941, when it was expected that women complete as much education was necessary and then fill the space of wife and mother. There was never any question that this was the natural order of things.

Mum was a bit of a rebel and excelled at school and wanted to study further. She did just that while working after school with her family. Marian then met Dad and filled the obligatory position as that wife and then mother. She followed dad around as he crossed the country for work, setting up house at every new destination and then moving when the time arose.

In her stoic fashion when Dad decided to start his own business, she was the pillar behind him ensuring that the house, kids and paperwork was always done. She made things look effortless. When the family opened the dog kennels, she took the position next to my Dad and together they built an empire, a name, and a reputation in the industry that still to this day holds great power.

When Dad got sick, mum stepped up and even went as far as getting a driver's license. She never bothered before because Dad would always drive her. To see this woman evolve as the times changed and simply just morph into whatever was required by her husband and family was awe-inspiring!

The expectation was always that Mum was mum, she was the support crew, the pit crew, the warm-up act to the star crew.

Because of outdated gender expectations, the assumption that mother knows best combined with cultural demand that fathers should be the provider and breadwinner, we've contributed significantly to the dichotomy that makes it easier for fathers to have children than it is for children to have a real father.

We need to stop framing parenting as something that only affects women. For some reason parenting seems to be the last bastion that we haven't had a concerted effort to remove the gendered assumptions of a bygone time from.

I love to sit and listen to Mums stories of our youth and how her and dad traversed through life as an unbreakable team, a partnership in all sense of the word. Never a decision was made without some form of collaboration and agreement. I can only fully appreciate this dynamic now that I have Charlie and realise that I am in fact a product of these two people that had no preconceived idea of what the societal norms dictated. They simply filled the roles as they were required. Let's be careful not to denigrate other choices, some mums choose to stay at home, they choose the full-time mum role just as I would embrace the roll as a full-time stay at home dad. Given a choice, this is what true equality is all about.

We need to stop framing men's mental health as somehow their failure to engage with services that clearly aren't designed, delivered or encouraging for those who need it the most. Failure to grasp these failures and stop the victimisation and criticism of vulnerable men will see women impacted as an unintended consequence. Women don't simply become mothers.

WE ALL BECOME PARENTS!

Sadly, women's drive for equality has the handbrake on, as evidenced by the trolling I receive ad nauseam telling me I'll never understand what true love is because I'm not a mother and never carried my daughter for nine months and how every child, especially MY daughter needs her mum?

Until women call out this language and outdated gender expectations and realise the dismissive disservice they are doing not only to fathers, but to all parents. Parents who may be adoptive, step or foster, conceive through surrogacy, same sex parents and the children of these parents who receive love without having been carried for nine months in their loving, devoted and besotted caregiver's womb regardless.

Somehow, I, we, and they, could NEVER understand what it's like to be a mother, yet somehow, they can speak with great clarity & confidence to others experience and the lesser extent of OUR love?

Just as I implore and expect men to call out and condemn sexist, misogynistic, bigoted or biased language and behaviour, we really need women to step up and do the same. Until men are seen as co-equal, competent, and important as parents, the handbrake on the drive for true gender equality will hinder our progress.

If it were not for the separation from Charlie's mum I would have reverted, as many men do, to being the second adult in the room – the helper, the assistant, deferring to Mum for anything and everything.

Leaving a laundry list of requirements for their partners when going to lunch with their friends, instructing the father on how to 'put a nappy on the right way', laughing at the outfit choice that Dad has selected, all point to maternal gatekeeping.

Mothers being cast as the primary caregivers for more years now than dinosaurs roamed the earth, places an undue amount of stress and pressure on the mum to be constantly on, constantly in-tune and aware of their children's every move, every need and every nuance. Naturally, Mums will be more inclined to be able to predict and offer care and comfort to the child.

Research shows that the more the mother exhibits maternal gatekeeping traits the more the partner allows the mother to continue to care exclusively for the child causing the partner to have less confidence in their ability to be able to care or contribute to the care of the child. This causes frustration for the mum as she feels that she does everything and the partner feels isolated and neglected for not being included in what should be a very special and bond-forming time in a young family's journey.

> I've come to realise that the best times during my days are those where the amount of time spent doing them isn't a consideration. These times and the sense of alignment with the moment only comes from being truly present and grateful in the moment.

I can only imagine how exhausting and frustrating it must be to monitor your children and micromanage your partner. It is usually chalked up to 'only a mothers love' or 'mother knows best'.

I so understand that feeling Mums have toward the children; the unconditional, unbelievable, and unmeasurable love. The very thought of something happening to them sends you into a cold sweat. I re-read these words now and all they are, are words on paper. It is so hard to describe the feeling that you feel when you look at your little treasures while they sleep and you trace their little rose-bud lips, you can see every little eyelash and the cute little button nose with a slight sprinkle of tiny light freckles over their little rosy cheeks. The ebb and flow of their breaths as they lose themselves in their little dreams; the dumpy little fingers holding onto the blanket and the warm baby breath as you put your head close.

I know what that feels like, and this is because Charlie does not have a present and involved mother. Now Mums think about all the fathers that are missing those very special moments. Moments that can never be recaptured, moments that disappear in a blink of an eye.

There is an undeniable feeling of utter and complete love for these little humans that you had a hand at creating.

Maternal gatekeeping should not by any means be perceived as a deliberate action on behalf of the mother, it is simply a role that they slip into based on the family dynamic. While the father is working to support the family, it has been traditional for mothers to take the time off work and be the primary care-giver and their controlling and management of the father's involvement is not preconceived.

The mere act of maternal gatekeeping contributes to the outdated gender expectations and the gender division of family responsibility.

Becoming a father so late in life and having the sudden change in the family dynamic was truly a blessing; I was never burdened by knowledge. I remember the old Doctor Spock books that seemed to be a mother's go-to for everything child based. These books recorded the development through pregnancy and then through every documented and proposed milestone described within a few months of the child's life. A first-time parent would religiously refer to this manual – and any other popular literature of its kind – tutoring and hoping that their children would reach the mark before (because we all believe our children as above average) or at least on time. The worry and consternation when they did not would leave parents sweating and pacing hoping that their child was indeed 'normal'.

I never knew what I should, shouldn't, could, couldn't, would or wouldn't do. I just had a connection with this little person. She was the other side of the puzzle piece. We just fitted together like a proverbial hand in glove.

Our days were filled with adventures. We were very fortunate enough to go to Disney World in Hong Kong when Charlie was just four years old. Just her and I jumped on a plane and headed off into the blue yonder and went on an adventure of a lifetime.

We were standing in a line listening to some street performers and Charlie, in all of her four-year-old fearlessness, walked into a group of dancers and started dancing along with them, much to the delight of the onlookers. I watched and started to well-up (yes, another cry) thinking about how I was always so worried that she was missing out, that she would not be complete without a mum, that I could not possibly give her everything that she could need and that I would somehow fail her and she would resent and hate me. But there was this little girl, this absolute perfect little human having the best time of her life, looking straight at me with those piercing blue eyes and smiling with every fibre of her body. I knew that I could not be doing such a bad job of the parenting thing. I think of how I would have missed this if we had been in a traditional family unit.

Allen and Hawkins (1999) identified three dimensions of maternal gatekeeping:

- *Standards and responsibilities*, when a mother does not want to relinquish childcare responsibilities and will take charge, institute unwavering standards and have strict control over the father's participation on the child/ren's life.
- The second dimension is *maternal identity confirmation* which refers to the external validation that the mother feels compelled to chase to affirm her maternal position and

- The third dimension is *differentiated family roles* that refers to the clear division of labour divided into the current outdated gender roles.

I remained single for five years by choice, to ensure a stable environment for Charlie as the thought of Charlie becoming attached to someone and vice versa with no real prospect for a long-term relationship wasn't something that I was willing to risk. I finally met my amazing partner and after a long courtship with lots of begging and pleading, mainly on my behalf. I still remember vividly the first weekend we spent together as a family. Charlie calling for my partner instead of me; how wounded and marginalised I felt. Suddenly, it felt like I had gone from the most important person in the world to an odd sock. In the flurry that happens when arriving at my partners house for the weekend, I am simply relegated to butler duties of dragging in the suitcase, toys, clothes, books and whatever else Charlie and Robin will be amusing themselves with. In a whirlwind of catch up stories and plans and schedules for the weekend activities, I am left to make supper and set the table.

In those five years, when it was just Charlie and me, I found great identity, purpose and agency in being solely responsible not only for the practical day to day parenting but also for the decision making and mental load, but also the realisation of the extent to this change of self-perception only became glaringly apparent when the change in family dynamics happened.

Many of the fathers that I talk to all feel that they are deliberately denied access to the children as they are seen as bumbling fools or incapable of doing the smallest task without being micromanaged or given clear and precise instructions on how things are to be done. One father told me of a time when his partner wanted to go out with her girlfriends on a Saturday and left him a list of tasks covering both the childcare responsibilities and the household task with a suitable time for the task to occur and approximate completion time and an asterisk * for things that she knew she would have to check when she returned home.

Another study also mentioned that maternal gatekeeping is a result of the women's fear of losing responsibility and power. This fear can affect a woman that is coming out of the workforce or one that has not been in the workforce, affirming their self-esteem and validating them as women, as a contributor to the family, and more importantly, relevant.

The amount of pressure that is placed on mothers to be perfect is staggering and this pressure usually comes from themselves. The expectation that they are required to be the cake-baking, child minding, school run, lashed and make up goddess is eye opening. Being lucky enough to be allowed in the fold of mothers, I have been privy to the vulnerability that women feel when they observe others that seem to have it all together and how unsuccessful they feel. If they are great mothers, they feel that they should be able to be great mothers and have a successful career and have a perfectly manicured house and garden too!

In another study by De Luccie, 1995; Fagan & Barnett, 2003, maternal gatekeeping was seen as a negative aspect to fathers' direct involvement in childcare and domestic duties. In the study it was found where there was a high probability of maternal gatekeeping, fathers that did participate in childcare and domestic duties, the mother would downplay or underestimate the father's involvement.

Fathers now have to step up and play a more active role in both the amount of time that they dedicate to childcare and the actual involvement in housekeeping tasks. The only way that women can achieve true equality and for them to ensure that they have the required self-esteem for them to feel that they are an integral and contributing part of the family unit is to have their partners step up and take on more responsibilities, but not as babysitters or assistants, rather as partners.

The fact that our household does not have the prejudicial gender roles, I believe will educate Charlie to understand that there is no division of responsibility.

While in lockdown Charlie decided that she wanted to bake a cake for the ambulance workers to thank them for their hard work while we were all safe at home. Even after the last cake making fiasco of 2018 for her seventh birthday party, she still wanted to attempt fate again. We both spent hours pouring over designs, online shopping for all of the required baking paraphernalia and just the right colours and additions to make our creation. There was a great deal of excitement deciding on all aspects of the Easter Bunny that we were about to create. After dinner on a few nights, we got the laptop out and did some searches and did copious amounts of rudimentary sketches of what this little field creature should look like, while I tried to simplify the design, Charlie continued to add elaborate designs and additions.

I remember the day clearly when we were due to bake. We were washing dishes together looking out over our back yard and our two wildly fat guinea pigs were grazing the lawn. Looking out the window, I said to Charlie that we really needed to get the lawn mowed and the weeds pulled before we lost our Chihuahua in the grass. We decided that after the breakfast dishes we would tag team and get the yard done.

Off we went, Charlie and I as a team. After starting the mower, Charlie mowed the lawns, with a little help when it was time to turn the mower around. There are no jobs that are reserved for gender in our home and there is no one else but the two of us.

I was listening to a podcast the other day and they mentioned that there was a study done where a whole bunch of adults were asked to draw a depiction of a leader, unsurprisingly the vast majority of the adults – both males and females drew the leader as a male. Someone else loved the concept and took it a bit further asking children to draw a leader with most drawing their mothers, teachers, some fathers and even drawing themselves. What does this teach us? Children are the intelligent ones; they do not seem to see leadership as gender based but rather as influence based.

Equality means recognising our differences and holding everyone to the same standards and requirements.

Women shouldn't be made to feel that their children are getting second best because the father is the primary caregiver. Men need confidence to step up and be supported in their desire to be more connected, and more respected for what we contribute to our children's lives.

WHO KNEW?

Chapter Ten

A level playing field

"I think a lot of it is social constructs around expectations that are placed on us, by others.
We've focused our equality initiatives on the finish line without a concurrent focus on the starting line."

Michael Ray

We're all so busy as parents that sometimes it's easy to slip into an authoritarian style of parenting with its orders, demands of certain behaviours, and coercive reward and punishment regime more suited to training puppies than little people who can easily become preoccupied with seeking approval from the most important person in the world.

My parenting, at its best, is questionable.

I want Charlie to question everything except her value and worth and recognise when others don't. The quality of her life will depend on the quality of the questions she asks so we welcome dissent, discussion, and compromise because the thought of anyone controlling, manipulating or coercing her breaks my heart so we need to practice this now so it becomes her default setting.

What does it mean to be a father in a time where the base identity of a 'male' is being challenged, even called 'toxic'?

"The current focus on toxic masculinity has many men feeling consciously and unconsciously that they are toxic as individuals," psychotherapist Carla Manly explains, "This result is a sense of wariness and constant fear. This fear – much of it unprocessed – can lead to detachment from relationships. This, of course, can lead to a sense of loneliness that feeds a general sense of unhappiness."

Never make people feel unsafe expressing their negativity. Negativity thrives in isolation.

We could make people think there's something wrong with them for not simply 'choosing' happiness and shame is negativity's enabling best friend.

Let's accept, support and champion the heck out of each other and their perspectives, because we're all in this together!

I often find myself pointing out to those naysayers who like to cite the plethora of laws, legislation, programs, initiatives and advocates that are aimed at and working towards ensuring equal opportunities and equitable outcomes for all, that it's virtually impossible to grasp these hard-fought opportunities and rights when your hands are already full of carrying the extra responsibilities and outdated gender expectations of a bygone time.

We've focused our equality initiatives on the finish line without a concurrent focus on the starting line.

A focus on opportunities without a consideration of responsibilities is well meaning, however, it has limited chance of achieving the long-lasting structural changes that are needed. It's akin to parking the ambulance at the bottom of the cliff.

A level playing field, a removal of handicapping and an even starting point is needed to achieve equality, inclusion, diversity of people and of choices for all.

Most of the equality initiatives that we are still championing today were conceived and constructed in a time when men were considered as uninterested, unsuitable, incapable or all three to raise the next generation, and therefore, we are focused on enabling women to enter the workforce whilst maintaining their caring responsibilities, without a concurrent focus on enabling dads sharing the care because of the misguided perception. This is simply adding more pressure and has in fact reinforced and enabled the status quo of women doing the majority of the caring. More of the same has limited prospects of breaking the inertia or recruiting the necessary stakeholders to advance equality in any meaningful way. If we continue, we are simply treating the symptoms of inequality and not the cause; begin at the beginning and hold men equally responsible for raising the next generation by enabling, encouraging, and expecting them to do so.

Privilege depends on which lens you are looking through – if it is the age old one focusing on career, then yes, men are privileged, however if you look at men through a lens of caring responsibilities then they are the ones that are disadvantaged. This lens still sees men as 'men at work' rather than 'working dads', this moves the scales of inequity to the opposite side. Men now want to have flexible work arrangements that sees them not having to make excuses or fabricating the reason that they are leaving for family responsibilities.

Why is it that when men want to step up and take responsibility there are naysayers? Our clarity through crisis as a society happened with Covid, the forced change in our circumstances saw men being able to take the bite of the family apple and feel what it is like to be actively involved in their kids' lives.

WHO KNEW?

Chapter Eleven

Inclusion means everyone, right?

"If we don't intentionally include,
we will unintentionally exclude.

Gender inequity is structural and systemic inequality affects women and men. It's not only about the jobs we hold, but it's also about cultural expectations and assumptions about family values."

Michael Ray

Today's workplace and family are all in flux, yet most of our social norms were set in a bygone time that can be witnessed in business and home structures.

"The family, as the fundamental group in society and the natural environment for the growth and well-being of all its members and particularly children, should be afforded the necessary protection and assistance so that it can fully assume its responsibilities within the community." ~ United Nations Convention of the Rights of the Child.

"An association of people, whether natural, legal or a mixture of both, with a specific objective. Company members share a common purpose and unite to achieve specific, declared goals.'

~https://www.marketingtutor.net/

Surprisingly the parallel between the definition of a family and a business are incredibly similar.

The cultural and societal change needed to drive the structural and systematic reforms required to facilitate true equality begins within families, within the home and then spills into the organisation.

We need to begin at the beginning and enable, encourage, and expect men to be held equally responsible for raising the next generation with equality being the default for that generation, rather than trying to manufacture equality as an outcome.

Gender inequality is structural and systemic inequality that affects women and men. It's not only about the jobs we hold, but it's also about cultural expectations and assumptions about family values.

Until men are enabled, encouraged, and expected to be equally responsible for raising the next generation, HR departments will struggle with any meaningful change.

Within an organisation there is a structure that is chosen to facilitate the growth and success of the business based on the values and principles of the founding members.

Regardless, if a company provides a service or a product, it will start with an idea, an idea that is discussed, changed, altered, and worked until it aligns with the principles, values and ethos of the founding members. The message that is devised is proudly used to market and grow the business.

The human element will ultimately determine the success or failure of your business. These individuals – and this applies to sole traders – will be responsible for every facet of the business and ultimately the customers overall experience. This human element is largely overlooked as being a liability rather than the assets they really are.

There has been an incredible push to institute human resource policies that try and regain the importance of the human element in a business. With legislation being passed there is a requirement for policies and procedures to be put in place, to be filtered to the employees and to ensure that all of the relevant operations boxes are ticked.

These policies ensure that the companies are seen as, 'family-friendly' which broadly implies that the company endorses a balance between work commitments with family responsibilities. However, in most cases it seems to be relegated to simple lip-service. How many organisations are taking the time to action these policies and procedures and get the C-suite to actively live them, set examples, and encourage a culture of being an 'equal opportunity employee'.

Similarly, in a family, it starts with the founding members that have similar values and principles and as life happens, the plans for growth and development grow and goals are altered. This could be the starting of a family, purchasing of a family home, buying a new vehicle and a myriad of other life-changing decisions.

Unintentional policies and procedures are put into place that allow for the smooth transition to the new phases of growth as required.

As parents we learn things which are incredibly valuable in the workplace. For example, how to see and draw out the best in another, kindness, compassion and patience, efficiency, and time management. All skills which are important in team building and leadership roles, not just at home.

Staff turnover, burnout, and the impact of less-than-optimal family life will affect performance, culture, and the bottom line of any organisation and thus, the need for the synergy between these two habitats.

It really isn't rocket science. Human Resources departments need to be considered as a profit centre rather than simply a regulatory or administrative process of business. Recovery is as vital for athlete's performance as is the training load and stimulus. Good human resources is as vital as recovery to an athlete or team — it optimises organisations performance directly.

The outdated expectation that employees are still expected to work the standard 40 hour a week within set hours is a truly outdated model and perhaps employers have a role to play in better accommodating parents.

With the world-wide pandemic and lock down there has been a crisis point for organisations to become more flexible and there is no reason, if it worked for this period, that it is not something that can be offered in the future in some way or form. Understandably there will be a call for some form of interaction with the organisation and its other employees, and flexi-hours. Rotational team hours are all options that have proven to be effective.

Our families aren't an interruption or hindrance to our careers. The need to provide for our families is the very reason our careers are important to us.

For too long workplaces have shaped, even dictated family roles and dynamics, aided by the misguided and divisive practice of classifying parents as 'primary and secondary caregivers'. This has the potential to diminish, devalue and even damage the relationship not only between fathers and children, but also between mothers and employers.

It has allowed workplaces to be willfully blind to parent's – mainly fathers – caring responsibilities and a major motivation for our careers.

Family friendly workplaces should never be the exception. They MUST be the rule. Our children and our society are dependent on it.

A crisis of any kind has the ability to focus our mind with laser-like precision onto what truly matters. It might seem with COVID that our lives have suddenly become a burning house that we've built, and we're being asked, "What are you prepared to rush in to save?"

What does your answer say about you? What are YOUR values and priorities when you strip away ego, fear and facade in this moment of crisis?

With this GIFT of absolute clarity, focus and reflection, ask yourself –

Are they your values you've been living?

Let's not forget the 'Renaissance' followed the plague. The Renaissance was a period in European history marking the transition from the Middle Ages to Modernity.

Say it. Show it. Live it!

In these uncertain times, more than ever, we need to focus on our children's wellbeing and state of mind more so than their academic advancement. The priority should be on connection, not correction or control. It's our rock-solid attachment that allows our children to trust us, allows us to guide them.

It will be infinitely easier to make up any lost ground academically than to try and rebuild or repair a fractured relationship once we're through this temporary situation. Research shows the presence of one loving, consistent adult can buffer the worst effects of stress and adversity for kids. Says Gunnar, from the University of Minnesota: "If the parent is present and the relationship is secure, basically the parent eats the stress."

Gender doesn't matter.

Maybe this is a time for a consideration of our society going forward, a re-examination of who we are, of ourselves, and the values we assign to things? Some of our greatest achievements have sprung from difficult times. Growth, change, and resilience come from our struggles not our comfort.

Suddenly the need to support others and the realisation of how interdependent we all are on each other is front and centre. The vulnerability of our aged, our frail, of our families and those in our community less fortunate than us is abundantly clear, because suddenly, their daily reality is ours.

I'm hopeful that from this testing time we will emerge with an appreciation of the need for a different approach, a different perspective and genuine sense of gratitude.

Let's make the most of this opportunity by starting with the realisation of the house of cards we have been living in and make this a seminal moment for a better way of family, of life, work and community. Helping others is the only way to help ourselves.

As parents we can either manipulate our children's behaviours or we can inspire them by our examples, values, and actions. As parents and as leaders we should ground ourselves in values that last like love, empathy, honesty, work, responsibility, fairness, generosity, respect for others.

> Some parents hold their kids to a standard they've got no right to hold them to as far as empathy and their sense of self.

We won't get it right every time. We'll make mistakes like we all do. But if we listen to the truth that's inside ourselves, even when it's hard, even when it's inconvenient, our children will notice. They'll gravitate towards us and imitate our examples.

Our crisis has made each family real, with zoom meetings being the norm, suddenly being invited into other homes has made us more human and more tolerant. The need to shush the kids and quiet the dogs is no longer an issue. The fact that we all have family around us and that this is essentially an integral part of us that we no longer fear to keep hidden.

When I speak with dads about the barriers and challenges, they can identify what is stopping them being the dad they want to be, workplaces and career paths are constantly being in top few stressors.

As there were ridged roles within organisations pre-Covid, we need to allow for organisations and parents to explore what benefits the organisation and the home. Organisations that support and facilitate the family lives of their teams will have a more focused, highly effective, and stable team.

There's a big difference between being 'in charge' and being 'a leader'.

As a parent I try to be a leader. Leadership is about giving away your authority to those you lead. Being a leader is about empowering and inspiring them with your example, encouraging them with an unwavering support and connection that fuels their confidence to stretch themselves without a fear of failure, rather than manipulating or coercing compliance and certain behaviours. As John Quincy Adams states, "If your actions inspire others to dream more, learn more, do more and become more, you are a leader."

It's a funny paradigm I find myself in as a solo dad to my daughter. My value to an employer is diminished because of my parenting obligations and my parenting capabilities are often dismissed or considered 'cute' because of my gender.

It's amazing the perspective I've gained. In the workplace I'm competing against men with no child responsibilities in an environment where that's normal. I'm able to understand what my daughter is going to face if things don't improve.

Diversity and inclusion tend to be lumped together as the modern buzzwords for organisations to appear 'aware' and 'woke' and are generally misinterpreted and conflated. To understand the definition is to understand how vastly different these terms are and how they can be used within an organisation to strive for equality. Inclusion requires that everyone within the organisation is valued and everyone is able to achieve complete integration and let everyone feel accepted and comfortable. Diversity is the variation of individuals that make up the organisation and includes age, ethnicity, gender, situation and circumstance.

Diversity does not indicate inclusion.

Suddenly working from home and flexible working conditions have gained momentum because men are included and invested.

Some are striving for a workplace program, an initiative, a piece of legislation or some equality avenging hero to deliver equality to society, yet somehow, we don't work for it, prioritise or demand it in our own home or in our own relationships or in our jobs.

When an organisation has a culture that these men are bragging about working eighty hours and that they haven't seen their kids for three weeks they need to be encouraged to find that balance and realise that the reason they work is for their families and not to avoid their families.

I often hear how Dads don't have time to exercise. Well, why not exercise WITH your kids. Exercise doesn't have to be at the gym. Get out and kick the ball and run around and challenge them. They will love it. The school run, make it a thing where you can chat, play games in the car. It is the moments between the moments that often get overlooked. It's the fifteen minutes in the morning and fifteen minutes first thing when you get home and thirty minutes after dinner. That is all it takes.

It doesn't have to be magical weeks away at the beach. Until workplaces realise that and why the reason our careers are important to us, apart from satisfaction and mental stimulation, all the rest of it is to provide for our families.

They're going to have high turnover in staff. They're going to have distracted staff members. If employees are struggling at home, they won't be able to perform well at work. If their marriage is struggling because they are committing too much time and focus to work because of being under pressure, you're going to end up with burnout and mental health issues. And then if a divorce happens, employers are stuck with an emotionally, ill-equipped employee that is unable to be productive.

For too long workplaces have shaped their family dynamics rather than the other way around. None of the top-down initiatives are going to be able to be taken up because all of these opportunities now for moms or women where they can achieve all of this equality will be moot. *How are they going to carry that opportunity with both hands when they're still carrying the load at home because dad's workplace hasn't moved with the times?*

Mums now have the opportunity to work outside of the home. I think a lot of the initiatives have simply added more pressures. Even though it may be easier, they are still expected to maintain the work inside of the home.

I keep telling Charlie the thing she needs to realise is that nothing ever gets easier, the weight never lighter, the distance never gets shorter, the sums, spelling or understanding don't suddenly become clear. But, you become better. They stay the same, but you change, adapt, and improve to be able to do what you couldn't, how cool is that?

You're literally building a better version of yourself by trying to do all the things you can't do! As a strength and conditioning coach one of the rock-solid principles to improve performance is over stretching, pushing someone just out of their zone of performance for short periods and then allowing recovery. If these periods are extended for too long, it becomes a negative stimulus in results in over training and can set the whole program backward by months.

Trust is maintained when values and beliefs are actively managed. If parents and companies do not actively work to keep clarity, discipline, and consistency in balance, then trust starts to break down.

Leading or parenting, means that others or our children willingly follow you — not because they must, not because they are paid to, but because they want to.

WHO KNEW?

Chapter Twelve

'Ubuntu'

"Ubuntu is the simple concept of humanity,

oneness and togetherness."

Michael Ray

Ubuntu!

This is a colloquialism for the Zulu saying, *'Umuntu ngumuntu ngabantu',* which literally means that a person is a person through other people.

In African philosophy the idea of community is one of the pinnacle building blocks of society. Ubuntu is the simple concept of humanity, oneness, and togetherness.

The modern concept of this very African term and belief was first made popular by Archbishop Desmond Tutu is his renowned book, 'No Future Without Forgiveness'. He describes a person with Ubuntu as, "open and available to others, affirming of others ... has a proper self-assurance."

My partner is South African and she's explained the origin of Ubuntu. The belief in a universal bond of sharing that connects all humanity. She grew up in the apartheid era and was fortunate enough to be in Africa when they joined in Ubuntu to make a change for the better. The uniting of a nation.

The country stood in unity. They were not looking for allies but stood together as one to initiate and drive change. Reference to the past was just that − a reference to the past − and a driving force for the future. Ubuntu moves away from blame, away from condemnation and concentrates on unity.

No, you haven't suddenly fallen down a rabbit hole and are now learning about South African history. I certainly have not hung up my 'Solo Dad' tag and taken on 'historian' as a career. I do however relish reading about historic events that revolutionised how we think, and it makes me reflect on my interpretation of my life.

As a society we rightfully share complete outrage and object strongly to inequality, yet we do not strive to achieve it as a moral and legal principle together. Like the principles behind Ubuntu, it encompasses a stand against inequality and discrimination. It encompasses the ability to work together towards a common goal as a collective humanity.

So, what does Ubuntu have to do with the equality debate and how does it have relevance to this book? Clarity through crisis, our global crisis, came in the form of Covid 19, and one year on we are still in a state of flux and indecision.

What it did alter considerably was the family dynamic with the push to work from home, flexi-hours, zoom calls with dogs barking, kids running around in the background with no nappy on, home schooling in between and meetings with work dress at the top and PJs at the bottom.

I have said before and I will reiterate now that I do not speak for women and will never profess to understand the daily tribulations that they conquer. I can only report back on what I have been told as an honoury mum. The mums I speak to feel that the debate should not be about what men should be allowed or required to do but rather what women should rightfully be doing. It is not about men. It is about women. It is the perpetual debate as to who deserves what and how it needs to be achieved. Can we even agree what 'equality' means? Or are we influenced by the echo chambers that we find ourselves in, being fed information that affirms our current state of mind?

Jeremy Waldron, a New Zealand professor of law and philosophy who holds a professorship in New York University School of Law in 2015, spoke on the fundamental nature of human equality. He started his lecture by prompting those attending to look around and to note the differences between themselves and those around them. There was an eclectic mix in the audience of all ages, genders, social hierarchy, financial statuses and sexual preferences. The question then rang out, *In what sense are people equal?*

The resounding answer is NO, we are not all equal, but we all need to be TREATED equally, regardless of how, who or what we are. It is a fundamental right to be treated as you would treat others and how others are treated. *Is it then possible that this is not a binary choice? That people can be seen as equal and unequal simultaneously?*

There are two equality distinctions that may illustrate how we interpret the gender debate and almost create equality when looked at in combination. Shallow equality compares only the immediate contents that we find ourselves exposed to, and the conclusion of this immediate contents is based on our personal internal and external factors, whereas deep equality refers to when we compare contents based of primitive fields, like love, virtue and even suffering, and basically tells us things that are fundamentally wrong. How many times have I been told that I will never understand a 'mothers love' as I never carried my daughter for nine months, and I agree, I could never understand the feeling, the emotion, and the internal turmoil that a woman feels when carrying a child. However, I don't understand how the naysayers can speak with such clarity and confidence about the lesser intensity or depth of my love connection and devotion to my daughter as a father. This is what I speak of when we talk about deep equality. We also need to consider how this has the potential to dismiss the love of same sex parents who may have conceived through surrogacy. Regardless of gender, adoptive, step, foster parents, even grandparents, are being portrayed as less able to provide a complete version of love, devotion and dedication, simply because they did not carry the child. Does this put more pressure on women?

Equality flows from our personal experiences and the ever-changing landscape of our lives. As a married man with a family when Charlie was born and casting myself in the role as provider, disciplinarian, and brilliant executive assistant to Solo Dad of a two-year-old, sharply changed my focus, my energy, and my ideals to something that was completely foreign to me. The realisation that the outdated gender norms were indeed that – outdated, changed me. The ballet school once again changed what I had then sculpted to be my normal and changed me indelibly forever. With Charlie growing up and entering her tween years, once again, this has taken my acceptable norms and turned them on its head.

There is no fundamental cell that makes us equal. It is the patchwork of our lives that will assist us in solving the egalitarian issues. We have to feel our way forward; we have to change with the ever-changing landscape as we grow and change as a society.

"I Acknowledge, that outdated gender expectations and stereotypes often makes me the TARGET of judgement and stigma. That's on them. What I will never accept, is that I'm a VICTIM of those who judge and stigmatise. That's on me!"

As a strength and conditioning coach, I used to coach my athletes that they would be going up against people that trained differently, were genetically or substance enhanced, who had participated in the sport for longer, but the sport had one conclusion – to see who the best was. This is achieved through strict policies in sporting boards to monitor drug use, to monitor all the participants throughout their training and competitive lives. This evened out the playing field and ensured that there was an element of equality.

It is in these policies that we are falling short. In February 2019, there were thirteen states in America that banned asking for salary history in interviews. This is one of the best moves to make to correct the wage gap. Why? By relying on someone's salary history simply perpetuates the wage gap by using this as an indication as to what a suitable salary would be. Why not simply pay what the salary band for that position requires? In Australia it is still acceptable to ask this, however, it falls within a very grey area and most prospectives are now asked what their salary expectation is. This however once again could fuel the pay gap. In general, as women are paid less than men, the expectations are set by previous earnings and the subsequent feeling of not being deserving of any better.

In Australia we have the Equal Opportunity Act 2010 and the Anti-Discrimination Act 2004 that protects unjust or prejudicial treatment of different categories of people, so we in effect have the policies that I referred to above that are explicitly there to protect. However, *if we are failing in the equality debate, how does this not lead us to the culture that we as a society have perpetuated?*

When I started this chapter, I mentioned the worlds crisis being Covid 19 and the change in the flexibility of the workplace. This pandemic has seen dads been given the opportunity to be more involved and present in the daily operations of the home. They have had to share the workload and participate in the daily life of child rearing, of which many that I speak to are elated and excited at being given this opportunity.

So, with the focus being on women, more men are being disengaged. We are well aware of the motherhood penalty; the opposite side of the coin is the fatherhood forfeit.

Fathers forfeit time with their children, getting to see all those firsts, sometimes lasts and many of the in-betweens that encompass the amazing development from infant to child to adolescent. These are gone forever and on reflection one of the most common regrets when I speak with fathers, is this forfeit.

Caregiving and breadwinning seemed to be at opposite ends of the spectrum and irrespective of the caregiver status fatherhood is associated with breadwinning which in turn leaves less time for caregiving. Because of these constraints on caregiving men are often painted as the 'ideal worker'. They have little time for family commitments, and they are often perceived as committed and stable workers as they are driven by the responsibility and the need to provide enough income for their families.

As a single father I had the dichotomy of not having the outdated traditional gender division of labour with a partner while still needing to provide for my daughter. I thought stand-up comedy was difficult.

Try to read the room when you have mums and dads who think you are too 'fatherly' to do the caregiving properly, some even suggest adequately, and I am sure there are more than a couple that would even say safely, and then for some reason – it is mainly the fathers and employers – that think I am too 'motherly' to do the breadwinning with any success.

Most of the equality initiatives were conceived and drafted at a time when men were considered unable, unsuitable, uninterested or all three to be entrusted with raising the next generation, so the intent seems to have been to enable women to enter the workforce while maintaining their ability to continue with the majority of caregiving.

In my experience, these essential but misguided family friendly equality initiatives like flexible work schedules, paid leave, and subsidised childcare, promote work-family balance because they allow mothers to combine their work and family responsibilities while dad goes on his merry way, further entrenching him in the rigid fatherhood ideals.

This new fatherhood ideal sees men being torn between being the 'nurturing dad' and being actively involved in parenting and forming that connection with the children while taking on more of the caregivers' responsibilities and the 'provider dad' which is the traditional norm that remains deceivingly strong. As much importance as men place on being an involved, present and equal caregiver, often our workplaces put these desires out of reach. In many workplaces men are twice as likely as women to be refused flexible work requests. When they do avail themselves to these family-friendly initiatives they find themselves facing stigmas because their peers view flexible work pejoratively.

When we spin the coin of gender expectation and it lands on the side of the fathers, we see a distinct fear of negative repercussions for using these policies that were originally intended, promoted, and encouraged family friendly ideals. While dads still hold the provider dad mentality and embrace the new fatherhood ideal the pendulum swings as seen in a study that dads are now cutting into their leisure time to spend time with their children and not altering their work schedule.

There is a strong drive encouraging the use of quotas to address previous inequity on senior management positions, with no talk of a corresponding quota for men to take advantage of the equality initiatives.

Then on flip side, mothers are portrayed as less committed as caregivers as they strive to be a good provider. This judgment and stigma is commonly known as 'mum guilt' and is often self-inflicted as well as given social and cultural influences.

I have the unique perspective of being included as a peer in conversations involving groups of mothers and groups of fathers and the common theme is fear of failing their family, a fear of failing their partner, and more so a fear of failing themselves that causes an immense stress known as parental burnout.

Parental burnout is a reality of typical parenting stress and is defined as *a prolonged response to chronic and overwhelming parental stress* with parents becoming withdrawn, overwhelmed, and distant from their children while doubting their capacity and ability as a good parent.

The fathers I speak to often describe the difficulties in balancing their work and career ambitions and aspirations with fatherhood. More and more fathers are letting go of the idea of career advancement in order to ensure consistent and quality caregiving. Many have done so by switching careers, many have started their own businesses or simply reorganised, redesigned, reprioritised and even reinvented their lives as I did. Of course, there are many trade-offs. None of the men that I speak to who have embraced this new paradigm have described this experience as negative. Once they have realised and accepted their new reality for being physically present in their child's life, especially if they had previously been boxed into the outdated masculine assumption of a breadwinner with limited childcare involvement.

Archbishop Desmond Tutu describes the philosophy of Ubuntu as, "We think of ourselves far too frequently as just individuals, separated from one another, whereas you are connected and what you do affects the whole world." He also stated, "When you do well, it spreads out; it is for the whole of humanity."

It reminds us that no matter what we do affects family, friends and society. We need to think about our choices, and realise the impact it has on those around us. Why is parenting the last bastion of contemporary society that has not had the gendered lens and assumptions of a bygone time removed? Women simply do not become mothers and men don't just become fathers. We ALL become parents.

So, how do we balance the scale? How do we as men make space in the workplace to advance equality for women, for men, for Ubuntu?

My mantra is if we Enable, Encourage and Expect men to be held equally responsible for raising the next generation, this will create the space and opportunity for women in the workplace and provide our children with the many unique and important benefits that an involved and present father provides.

We Enable, through removing the gendered nature and assumptions of many of the current initiatives, throwing the primary and secondary caregiver classification into the rubbish bin of history, removing the assumptions of family structures within policies, pay superannuation as part of parental leave.

We Encourage, by highlighting the preponderance of unique vital benefits an involved and present father provides for his children's educational, social, psychological and behavioural outcomes. The flow on effects for equality and men's mental health.

Finally, I talk about my unique perspective of being a Solo Dad to a daughter and the challenges of being the Only Unicorn in the Village and how to Enable and Encourage contributions would have changed the experience.

My journey has only begun and the information that I glean from all of the individuals and organisations that I am in contact with is ever changing, morphing and dynamic. I am humbled and grateful that I am able to share this journey with Charlie, and with both being really new at this father-daughter thing and me thankfully being consciously incompetent and blissfully ignorant of what to expect the journey has unfolded exactly as it has and exactly as how it should.

To the tweens and beyond!

WHO KNOWS?

Phat Fatherhood Facts

A compilation of inspirational quotes and facts about fathers

Inspirational Quotes

"What makes you a man is not the ability to have a child — it's the courage to raise one." - Barak Obama

"One of the greatest things a father can do for his children is to love their mother." – Howard W. Hunter

"My father didn't tell me how to live. He lived and let me watch him do it." – Clarence Budington Kelland

"We need to show our kids that you're not strong by putting other people down — you're strong by lifting them up. That's our responsibility as fathers." - Barak Obama

"Fathers, like mothers, are not born. Men grow into fathers and fathering is a very important stage in their development." – David Gottesman

"Dads are most ordinary men turned by love into heroes, adventurers, story-tellers, and singers of song." – Pam Brown
"Children need models rather than critics." – Joseph Joubert

"A good father is one of the most unsung, unpraised, unnoticed, and yet one of the most valuable assets in our society." – Billy Graham

"Fathering is not something perfect men do, but something that perfects the man." – Frank Pittman

"My father gave me the greatest gift anyone could give another person; he believed in me." — Jim Valvano

"A great father is one whose children look up to him rather than away from him." — Richelle E. Goodrich, Slaying Dragons

"A dad is someone who wants to catch you before you fall but instead picks you up, brushes you off, and lets you try again." Author Unknown

Australian Father Phat Facts

In Australia, 1 in 5 single parent households are dads, single father and single mum households are increasing at 14% and 9% respectively every 5 years. This trend will see single mums in the minority eventually.

There are approximately 4.6 million dads in Australia, with an estimated 2.2 million dads currently with children aged under 18. Of these, approximately 156,000 are single-parent fathers, who look after 228,000 children, which averages at 1.5 kids for each single dad.

Stay at home dads in 2 parent households increased from 68,000 in 2008 to over 80,000 in 2011, while the percentage remains relatively small at 4% it represents a fascinating shift in our gender expectations. The fastest growing family demographic in Australia (ABS census) is single father households. Estimated to increase 40 - 65% by 2041.

The average age of a Dad with a newborn baby is now 33. The Northern Territory and Tasmania are home to our nation's youngest dads, with the median age of fathers at 31.5 and 31.7 years respectively at the child's birth. However, Victoria and the ACT have the oldest dads, with a median age of 33.7 years at birth.

ABS figures show that in Australia there are approximately 144,000 stay-at-home dads with dependent children. This means that of the 4.4 million dependent children in couple families where one parent is employed full time, 3% have a mother who is employed, while the father is not.

Stay-at-home father families tend to look different to stay-at-home mother families, with the most notable differences being that stay-at-home fathering happens later in life, when fathers and children are older, compared to stay-at-home mothering.

The small number of stay-at-home fathers suggests that, despite changes in attitudes toward involved fathering, and also increased employment participation among mothers, there are factors making this arrangement not workable for many families. This is in part likely to be related to financial constraints on families needing two incomes, but gendered parenting attitudes are also likely to play a part.

Trends in Fathers Employment in Australis 1991 – 2016

In Australia, fathers may request to work part-time hours, as a flexible work option, to assist in the care of children. However, they rarely do, and instead work in the full-time labour market, in which expectations about long work hours tend to prevail (Smyth et al., 2012)

	2001		2016	
	Partnered	Single	Partnered	Single
Full Time	74	45	77	53
Part Time	9	12	10	15
Away from Work	5	4	3	0
Unemployed	4	10	3	8
Not in Labour Force	8	30	7	24

Away from work includes those classified as employed but with work hours of zero or not stated.

The most common work arrangement for men for fathers that care for their children is flexible work arrangements.

The next most common is for fathers to work from home and is the arrangement that is on a steady increase.

There are very few fathers reported in part time employment due to a lack of available positions.

Modern Australian Family Facts

Grandparents commonly care for grandchildren, with 65% of grandparents aged 40–69 years doing caring duties at least once a week,

On the night of the 2011 Australian census, of children aged under 15 years old:

- o 71% lived with two biological or adoptive parents.
- o 19% lived with a single mother.
- o 2% lived with a single father.
- o 4% lived with a stepfather and a biological/adoptive mother.
- o 1% lived with a stepmother and a biological/adoptive father; and
- o 2% had other circumstances, including being a foster child or living with another relative.

The latest Australian Institute of Family Studies report (pre Covid) has 32% of single father households not in the workforce and only 15% able to work part time. With only 53% of single father households in fulltime work this staggeringly shocking disadvantage clearly shows framing #childcare as a 'Women's Issue' is not only counterproductive as it excludes the necessary stakeholders needed to advance the issue, but also a demonstrably wrong characterisation.

Equity Starts at Home

The socially acceptable nuclear family has been challenged with families taking on a myriad of forms and fathers coming in all forms and shapes: biological, foster, adoptive, same-sex, step, transgender, married, cohabiting, separated, divorced, and widowed. Male role models are also come in many forms; brothers, grandfathers, uncles, and male friends – having a 'good dad' in any of the above forms has a powerful and positive effect on children's lives and should be fostered and encouraged.

There has been a positive move towards recognising fathers as an integral part of the family unit as both a provider and a willing and eager parent, In the 1960's and 70's men were encouraged to be participate in parent groups, to be available during labour and to take a more active role in being a parent however the default setting seemed to be assistant to the pregnant partner before, during and after birth. All the pre and post birth information designed for fathers revolved around being that support! Remember those days when fathers would be taught breathing exercises and relaxation techniques to help the mother.

As we have progressed through the years there has been a sharp change in how fathers benefit from being involved and present, to the mother, child and for themselves and the potential to develop their identity as a parent.

Charlie's Chapter

'A funny look at dad!'

Charlie was asked a few questions about her Dad and these are her candid and funny answers – I think humour may run in the family.

My Dad is?

Not as funny as he thinks he is. His jokes are so lame and I ask people not to encourage him by laughing – I have to live with him!

My Dad isn't?

Selfish. Dad always includes me in all of the decisions at home. I even get to cook once a week. He won't let us have chocolate cake though (Charlie rolls her eyes here).

My Dad thinks?

He looks cool wearing shorts in winter – I just think that's weird!

My Dad does?

The chicken dance when the school song plays. He runs back to the classroom and starts a congo line and dances around with all of my classmates. I just hide under the table.

My Dad loves?

Watching anything to do with Donald Trump! That means I can't watch animal programs.

My Dad Dislikes?

Dad does not like leaving any chocolate left in the fridge. He thinks eating it all with me is a great way to make sure we eat all the junk so there is none for tomorrow.

My Dads Favourite?

Escaping from the ferrets when they are out and want to bite him. I am being sarcastic by the way.

My Dads Best Dish is?

Paella. Dad made a paella during lock down and we won a competition so he built my ferrets a cage with the winnings which was a Mitre 10 voucher.

My Dads Talent?

Being the best Dad, we do loads of stuff together and he always plays with me. He is a great vet assistant, and he watches vet programs with me. He takes me to the zoos, and we save loads of animals wherever we go. I know he loves all of our animals, even the ferrets that he says he doesn't.

References

A Content Analysis of Representations of Parenting in Young Children's Picturebooks in the UK. Sex Roles 65, 259–270 (2011).

Besemer S. A systematic review and meta-analysis of the intergenerational transmission of criminal behavior. *Aggression and Violent Behavior*,2017,37: 161-178

Fathering in Australia Among Couple Families with Young Children (Baxter & Smart, 2010)

https://aifs.gov.au/publications/family-matters/issue-87/children-poverty

Van der Horst, F.C.P., LeRoy, H.A. & van der Veer, R. "When Strangers Meet": John Bowlby and Harry Harlow on Attachment Behavior. *Integr. psych. behav.* **42,** 370–388 (2008)

Storey AE, Alloway H, Walsh CJ. Dads: Progress in understanding the neuroendocrine basis of human fathering behavior. Horm Behav. 2020

https://aifs.gov.au/publications/households-and-families

Gunnar, Frenn, Wewerka, & Van Ryzin, 2009; Miller, Seifer, Stroud, Sheinkopf, & Dickstein, 2006

Kaspiew et al., 2009

Donna Ferguson (2019) 'Highly concerning: picture books bias worsens as female characters stay silent' Guardian https://www.theguardian.com/books/2019/jun/13/highly-concerning-picture-books-bias-worsens-as-female-characters-stay-silent ; CLPE (2018) Reflecting Realities https://clpe.org.uk/publications-and-bookpacks/reflecting-realities/reflecting-realities-survey-ethnic-representation

Caldwell, Elizabeth F. and Wilbraham, Susan (2018) Hairdressing in space: Depiction of gender in science books for children. Journal of Science and Popular Culture.

Rosenberg, Jeffrey. & Wilcox, William Bradford. & United States. Office on Child Abuse and Neglect. (2006). The importance of fathers in the healthy development of children

Australian Human Rights Commission (HRC). (2014). Supporting working parents: Pregnancy and return to work national review. Sydney:HRC. Retrieved from www.humanrights.gov.au/sites/default/fi les/document/ publication/SWP_Report_2014.pdf

McLanahan S, Tach L, Schneider D. The Causal Effects of Father Absence. *Annu Rev Sociol.* 2013; 39:399-427. doi:10.1146/annurev-soc-071312-145704

DelPriore, D. J., Proffitt Leyva, R., Ellis, B. J., & Hill, S. E. (2018). The effects of paternal disengagement on women's perceptions of male mating intent. *Journal of Personality and Social Psychology, 114*(2), 286–302

ABS Gender Indicators, Australia, Sep 2017 (4125.0). 'Work and Family Balance'.

https://apolitical.co/en/solution_article/norways-daddy-quota-means-90-of-fathers-take-parental-leave

https://www.legislation.vic.gov.au/in-force/acts/equal-opportunity-act-2010/020

https://www.ag.gov.au/rights-and-protections/human-rights-and-anti-discrimination/australias-anti-discrimination-law

Gregory, Abigail, and Susan Milner. 2012. Men's Work-Life Choices: Supporting Fathers at Work in France and Britain? In Men, Wagem Work and Family. Edited by Paula McDonald and Jeanes Emma. London: Routledge, pp. 50–64.
Griffith, Annette K. 2020. Parental Burnout and Child Maltreatment During the COVID-19 Pandemic. Journal of Family Violence

Mikolajczak, Moira, James J. Gross, and Isabelle Roskam. 2019. Parental Burnout: What Is It, and Why Does It Matter? Clinical Psychological Science 7: page 1319

https://aifs.gov.au/aifs-conference/fathers-and-parental-leave

https://stories.clintonfoundation.org/the-spirit-of-ubuntu-6f3814ab8596

(https://mccrindle.com.au/insights/blogarchive/from-househubbies-to-onduty-dads-australian-fathers-are-actively-parenting)

(https://mccrindle.com.au/insights/blogarchive/from-househubbies-to-onduty-dads-australian-fathers-are-actively-parenting)

(https://mccrindle.com.au/insights/blogarchive/from-househubbies-to-onduty-dads-australian-fathers-are-actively-parenting)

(https://mccrindle.com.au/insights/blogarchive/from-househubbies-to-onduty-dads-australian-fathers-are-actively-parenting)

(https://aifs.gov.au/sites/default/files/publication-documents/stay-at-home_fathers_in_australia_0.pdf) **page 5**

 (https://aifs.gov.au/sites/default/files/publication-documents/stay-at-home_fathers_in_australia_0.pdf) **page 6**

(Source: Australian Population Census customised reports, 1991–2016Credit:Australian Institute of Family Studies 2019 (aifs.gov.au/copyright)

(https://aifs.gov.au/publications/modern-australian-family)

https://aifs.gov.au/publications/modern-australian-family#footnote-001

https://aifs.gov.au/media-releases/bringing-baby-fathers-not-always-able-share-load

State of the World's Fathers, produced by the MenCare campaign and led by Promundo, Sonke, Save the Children, Rutgers and Men Engage

(Plantin L, Olukoya A, Ny P (2011) Positive health outcomes of fathers' involvement in pregnancy and childbirth paternal support: a scope study literature review in Fathering: A Journal of Theory, Research, and Practice. Page 88)

(Plantin L, Olukoya A, Ny P (2011) Positive health outcomes of fathers' involvement in pregnancy and childbirth paternal support: a scope study literature review in Fathering: A Journal of Theory, Research, and Practice. Page 89

ABOUT THE AUTHOR

Michael Ray is a dad and single parent. He writes to inspire all with his experiences and struggles and his unconditional love for his daughter Charlie. Michael's journey has encouraged him to break the mould of male stereotypes, to overcome male stigmas, and allow men and fathers to focus on raising children with needed and expected ethics, and to allow our children to grow up with confidence and their own uniqueness.

When not writing Michael is blogging, podcasting or speaking and looking after the family's menagerie of animals. You can find him at www.michaelray.com.au

www.ingramcontent.com/pod-product-compliance
Ingram Content Group UK Ltd.
Pitfield, Milton Keynes, MK11 3LW, UK
UKHW041328090325
4914UKWH00019B/163